Small woven tapestries

Small woven tapestries

Mary Rhodes

B T Batsford Limited   London

First published 1973
Reprinted in paperback 1990
ISBN 0 7134 6375 9

Designed by Charlotte Baron, Libra Studios
Filmset in Monophoto Bembo (27ems 11 on 12 point)
by Keyspools Limited, Golborne, Lancashire
Printed in Great Britain
by Courier International Ltd
Tiptree, Essex
for the publishers
B T Batsford Ltd
4 Fitzhardinge Street, London W1H 0AH

Contents

Acknowledgment

I should like to thank all those kind people who have so willingly assisted me in the preparation of this book by lending me their woven panels to photograph. These are all members of my classes in the Greenwich and Eltham Adult Institutes of the ILEA, and without their great enthusiasm and industry the present work could not have been achieved.

My thanks are also due to the British Museum and the Victoria and Albert Museum, not only for permission to include photographs of some of the wonderful treasures from their famous collections of tapestry weaving from past ages, but also for the help given to me by certain members of their staff, when I was assembling the material for my purpose.

I am likewise indebted to Archie Brennan for sending me particulars of his metal-frame loom, to my kind friend Walter Barry for constructing me an actual loom to Mr Brennan's specification and to John Hunnex for supplying me with the excellent colour photographs.

Finally, I have to thank my husband for the remainder of the photographs, as well as for his assistance in typing the manuscript and reading and correcting the proofs.

Eltham 1973 MR

Introduction

The word tapestry is derived from the Latin *tapete,* which means a carpet, tapestry, hanging or coverlet, and was originally used to describe all types of wall hangings, furniture coverings or coverlets, whether they were woven fabrics or embroideries. From the sixteenth century onwards it was also applied to canvas work embroideries, with which it is to this day still popularly associated, as well as to Jacquard verdures and any other heavy woven or embroidered materials used as furniture coverings. It was not until the middle of the nineteenth century that the initiated came to use the word exclusively to describe the hand-woven material that was produced on either a high or a low-warp loom by weaving with soft woollen weft threads over hard warp threads and pressing the weft threads down so that they entirely covered the warp. This method of weaving produces a ribbed effect and causes slits to appear in the finished surface when areas of different colour meet along a line parallel to the warp.

It is this type of woven tapestry which is considered in this book. The development of the craft is traced briefly from primitive times, and suggestions are given for the weaving of simple tapestries on small rectangular frames in order to show how well this ancient craft can be used as a medium for modern ideas in design, by exploiting the special features of the technique of tapestry weaving rather than by adapting a preconceived idea to suit this technique. In making readers aware of the special qualities of tapestry weaving it is hoped, not only to help them to produce designs which are well suited to the medium, but also to give them a greater appreciation of the superb technical skill seen in the masterpieces of tapestry from the past.

Some people may well object to the idea of weaving small tapestries and maintain that tapestries should be designed purely as large wall hangings. They are, of course, essentially objects which make remarkably fine decorative adjuncts to the architecture of a building.

This is a reason why tapestry has renewed its popularity in modern times, for rooms in public buildings often have large undecorated wall spaces where tapestries can be hung with great effect. The work considered here, however, is that which can be achieved by those who cannot contemplate weaving large pieces of tapestry, who have no facilities for the use of large looms, but who wish to experiment with this craft. They can, by using a small frame, have all the pleasure of exploiting the special characteristics of tapestry technique and, although their pieces of work may not be suitable for the purposes of the modern interior decorator dealing with large houses and public buildings, they can make delightful pictorial panels for hanging in the smaller rooms in which very many people live today.

1 The development of tapestry weaving—an historical survey

The pre-Christian period

The origin of the craft of weaving is lost in the mists of antiquity, but there is no doubt that from the earliest times, when men began to live in communities, weaving has existed in some form or other, whether in the plaiting together of wattles or straw-like fibres to make protective fences against the intrusion of wild animals into human habitations, or later, after wool and linen had come into use, in the making of materials with which people might clothe themselves. This early weaving was, of course, very simple, with the weft material merely being taken over one warp thread and under the next. What we now think of as tapestry weaving was a natural development, the only difference being that in tapestry weaving the weft thread is not drawn too tightly, so that it can be knocked down to cover the warp threads completely.

Evidence of the existence of primitive tapestry weaving has been found in very many parts of the world, and in countries as far removed from one another as China, Peru and Egypt. In Egypt the earliest evidence of this kind is found in the *hypogeum* or tomb of Chnem-hotep at Beni-Hassan, where there is depicted on the walls a weaving loom, thought to date from the period between 2000 and 3000 BC. It is extremely simple, but it has all the essential parts for a low-warp tapestry loom. This is a loom in which the plane of the warp is horizontal, ie parallel to the floor. Some actual examples of woven tapestry have also been discovered in Egypt among the remarkable collection of ancient textiles which have been preserved down the ages in the tombs of the Pharaohs. Although these finds are far from numerous, they are of high quality and demonstrate that the craft was well-developed in ancient Egypt thousands of years before Christ.

The most important of these ancient Egyptian tapestries are three notable pieces from the grave of the Pharaoh Tuthmosis IV, which are now in the Cairo Museum. The largest of these, which is incomplete, is about 280 mm (11 in.) high and 435 mm (17 in.) wide, is woven in linen and has a plain white ground with an all-over pattern of lotus flowers in blue and red, alternating with papyrus inflorescences in blue, red, brown and yellow, outlined in black. The colours are still bright, particularly the reds and blues, but the browns have largely disappeared, leaving the warp bare. The back and front of the work are alike, with no threads left floating, and the weaving shows great freedom: when it has been found necessary to help the design, warps have been curved and the weft threads have been worked obliquely to them. As is usually the case with early Egyptian pieces, the texture is extraordinarily fine being, with sixty warp threads to 25 mm (1 in.), four or five times as fine as the Gothic tapestries of Western Europe, and the warp threads are much finer than the weft. These particular early examples of Egyptian woven tapestry are probably even older than the time of the Pharaoh Tuthmosis IV, in whose grave they were found: they seem to have been heirlooms, handed on to Tuthmosis IV by his father, Amenophis II, according to the customary practice of those times with such highly-valued objects. The most ancient piece bears the hieroglyphics of the Pharaoh Tuthmosis III and therefore probably dates from around 1500 BC. The only other extant pieces of Egyptian tapestry of this early period are a tapestry-woven robe and a nearly-complete glove, found in the tomb of the Pharaoh Tutankhamen (*circa* 1352–1344 BC) by Lord Carnarvon and Mr Howard Carter in 1923, and a linen girdle of Rameses III, which probably dates from about 1200 BC.

The fineness of the weaving in all the extant examples of ancient Egyptian tapestry undoubtedly resulted from their having been intended for use as decorative pieces of clothing and not as wall hangings, which would need to be much coarser and heavier, as were the great Gothic tapestries. No actual examples of ancient tapestry wall hangings of the same period have as yet ever been discovered in Egypt, but we can suppose from other evidence that such hangings were probably produced but have failed to survive to modern times.

1 A woven fragment with fringe. This is an intricate piece of Egyptian weaving of particular interest to the modern experimental weaver. *Victoria and Albert Museum* ▶

Ancient Greek tapestry

The only pieces of ancient Greek tapestry that remain are fragments of dress material now in the Hermitage Museum at Leningrad. They were taken from the tomb of the Seven Brothers in the Russian province of Kuban on the northern shores of the Black Sea and date from the third or fourth century BC. Just as in the case of ancient Egyptian tapestry the paucity of the actual remains does not necessarily indicate that there was not a great deal of tapestry produced in ancient times in Greece,

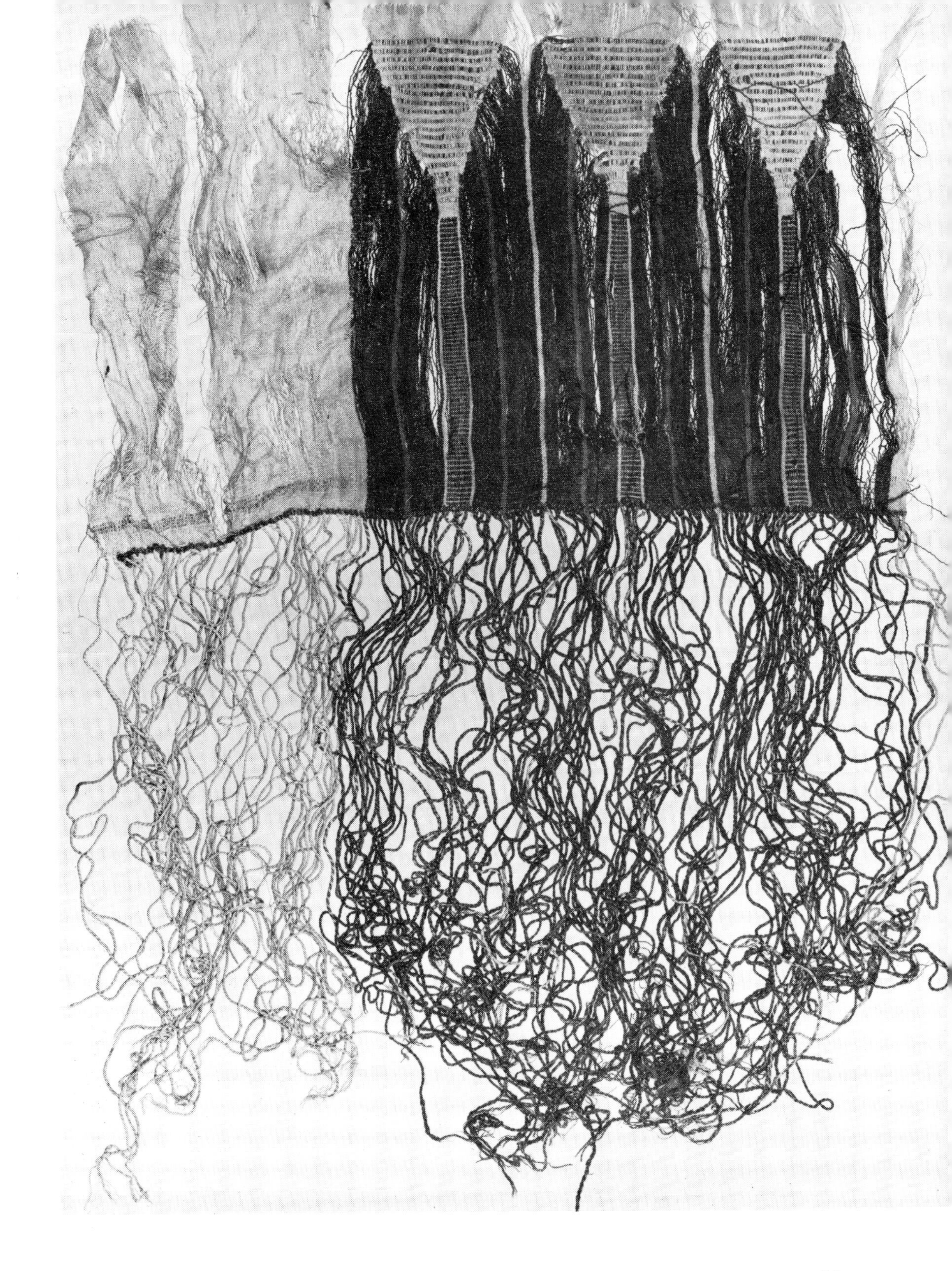

not only as dress material, but also for wall hangings, but the historian has to rely principally on the writings of ancient scribes and poets for his information.

Coptic tapestries

From the ancient Egyptians, who produced the excellent examples of tapestry weaving found in the tombs of their kings, the practice of this ancient craft passed on to their lineal descendants, the Copts. (Copt was a word derived from the Greek *Aigyptos* through the Arabic *Kipt*.) The Copts had early become Christians, but were subjugated in their own country in turn by Greeks, Romans (Egypt eventually becoming part of the Roman Empire in AD 30), and finally by the Arabs. It is, therefore, not surprising that the Coptic weavers reflect the influence of their various conquerors in the designs they use: Greek influence is seen in their early work, Roman influence appears later and then, following the Moslem conquest in the seventh century AD, Arab influence is apparent. Under the early Hellenistic influence Coptic tapestries reveal a naturalistic representation of themes from classical mythology and they portray in a realistic way human figures, animals, birds and plants, such as the grape vine (see figures 2 and 3). Later the naturalistic effect is gradually lost: at first in representations of the human face, for instance, it has been noticed that certain elements come to be accentuated; the eyes are depicted as particularly large and are outlined in black in a manner which bears comparison with Roman mosaics, by which the Coptic weavers were at this time probably being influenced (see figures 4 and 5).

In even later Coptic tapestries natural forms are used in a much less realistic manner: individual parts of human or animal figures, sometimes quite distorted, are often outlined in black or white and are thus separated from one another to form simple abstract units in an all-over pattern. During the declining years of the Roman empire and the early period of Moslem domination the Copts were subjected to persecution because of their Christian beliefs. They reacted to this situation by withdrawing into comparative isolation in their monastic establishments, and the designs of their tapestry work at this time reveal the movement away from the influence of classical culture and the development of a style of their own.

Although the technique of their weaving remains good during this period, the general quality of the design has deteriorated. After the Arab conquest Coptic art again came under external influence, and the tapestry designs show the usual Moslem predilection for abstract decorative forms (figure 12).

2 Coptic tapestry of a quail, fourth to fifth centuries. A charming little bird woven with extreme simplicity. The crosses which appear in the top, bottom and right-hand borders may be hidden Christian symbols. *Victoria and Albert Museum.*

3 A decorative square for a garment, fourth to fifth centuries. The centre motif is a lion, which is surrounded by a border of ornamental vine shoots. *British Museum*

4 Head of a woman, probably Venus, found at Akmin in Egypt, fourth to fifth centuries. This shows Roman influence in the large eyes and the heavy shadows on the face, and is reminiscent of the mosaics which were widespread throughout the Roman Empire. *Victoria and Albert Museum*

5 Head of a man, probably Adonis, found at Akmin in Egypt, fourth to fifth centuries. *Victoria and Albert Museum*

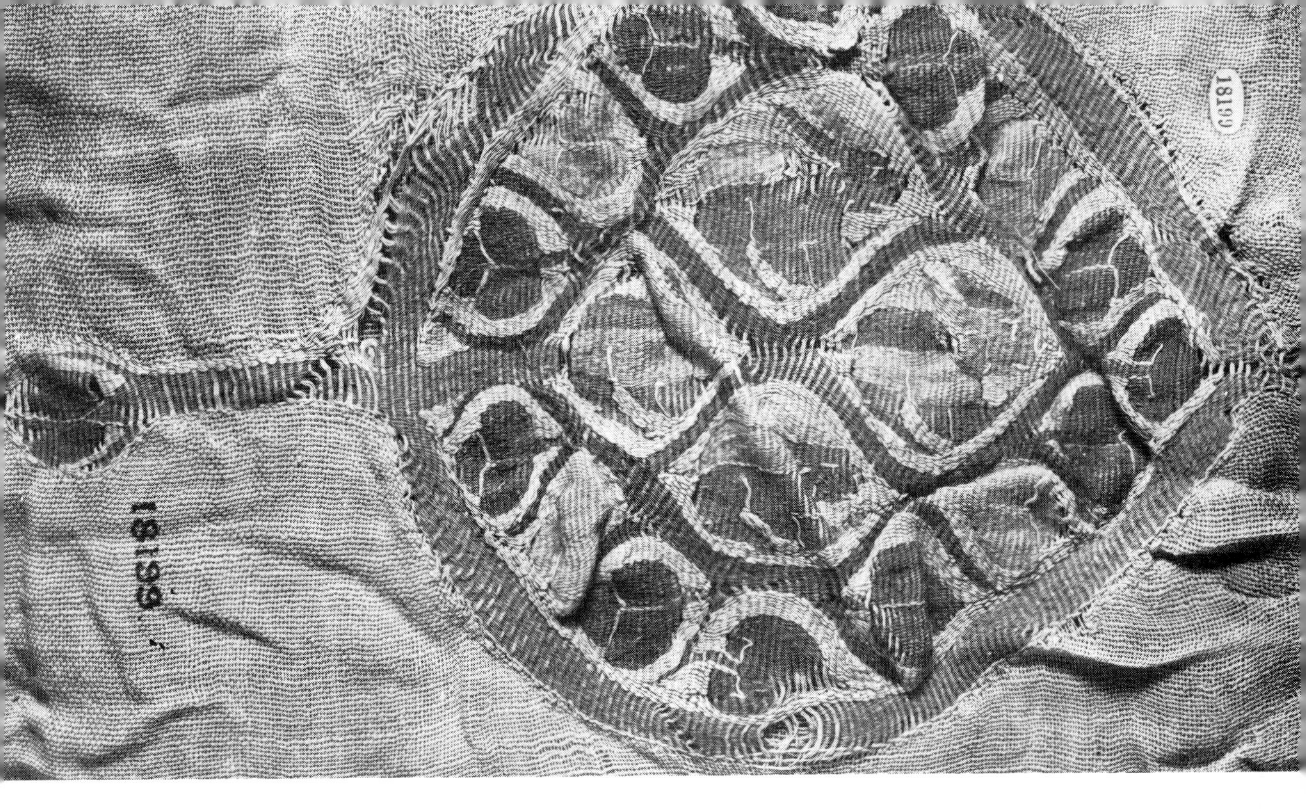

6 A leaf-shaped medallion which probably formed part of a garment. It shows hares and leaf-forms in an all-over pattern. The photograph shows clearly how the tapestry part is woven over double warp threads, whilst the warp threads are separated again when the plain weaving is continued, fourth to fifth centuries, *British Museum*

A large amount of the early Coptic tapestry weaving, like the ancient Egyptian fragments, consisted of ornamentation in the form of bands or panels worked into garments, many of which have been discovered in tombs throughout Egypt. A typical example of such work would be begun in ordinary shuttle weaving with linen thread, which would be carried on until the weaver wished to introduce a tapestry panel. At this point the weft thread would be changed, probably to wool, with linen for the highlights, and would be worked over two or more of the fine warp threads combined as one, the weaver beating down the weft, as is usual in tapestry weaving, and forming a ribbed effect. The ordinary shuttle weaving was continued to left and right of the tapestry panel and, when the latter was completed, the warp threads were separated again into their original number and the shuttle weaving proceeded across the full width of the loom. This method of weaving caused the tapestry insertion to be raised above the surface of the surrounding shuttle-woven linen material (see figure 6).

Sometimes it can be seen that tapestry-woven bands or panels of decoration have been applied separately to the surface of the material in a garment such as a tunic. This may mean that the tapestry panel or band had been woven separately and afterwards applied to the garment, but perhaps it is more likely that, when a garment which incorporated such sections of tapestry

7 An interesting small panel, showing a very lively little horse and rider in the centre circle with four kneeling figures in the corners, and four animals —two hares and two lions—at the sides. The background to the four figures is stippled and that to the animals is mottled, Egypto-Roman, fourth to fifth centuries. *British Museum*

weaving in its original construction began to wear, the tapestry panels, which were highly valued, were removed and applied to the surface of a newly-woven garment.

An outstanding characteristic of Coptic tapestry weaving was the extreme freedom with which the weft was used. Following a tendency, already noticed in the remnants of ancient Egyptian tapestry, to work the weft sometimes obliquely to the warp, instead of at right angles to it, the Coptic weaver often allowed his weft to follow the outline of the pictorial form he was working in such a way that the weft thread might take a direction diagonal to, or even almost parallel to the warp, as the weaver built up the mass of the particular form (see figures 2 and 6). In Western European tapestries the weft is only occasionally allowed to follow the shape of a rounded form, which is more often indicated by a series of steps or slits, but in Coptic work the weft may often follow the form depicted to such an extent that certain weft threads may almost make a frame around an area of weaving.

Another characteristic feature of Coptic tapestries is that the line of the warp threads is often so irregular that it gives an undulating effect to the ribs in the finished piece of work (see figures 3 and 6). This again is a feature which can be seen in the fragments of ancient Egyptian tapestry, and it probably resulted from the fact that the warp threads were kept very loose during weaving, although the exceedingly free way in which the weft was allowed to move obliquely to the warp would of itself cause some displacement of the warp threads to appear in a finished tapestry.

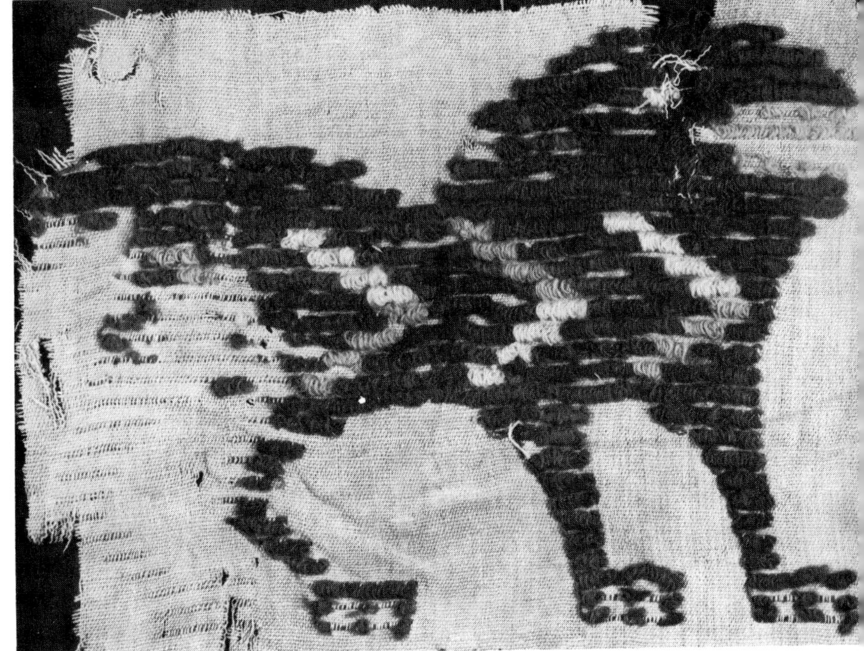

8 A decorative strip forming part of a garment. It is woven in wool on a linen warp and shows lions alternating with plant forms in a repeat pattern, fourth to fifth centuries. *British Museum*

9 (RIGHT) An animal, probably a lion, woven in the tufted technique, *c* fourth century. *British Museum*

10 (OVERLEAF) Decorative strip with birds, woven with wool and linen on one-ply linen warp, found in Egypt at Akmin, sixth to seventh centuries. *Victoria and Albert Museum*

Some Coptic tapestries also exhibit a looped technique in which the woollen weft is pulled through the linen warp to form short loops which are held in position by a row or two of plain weaving in linen. This produces a fabric with a rougher-looking surface, which in a completed panel gives the effect of mosaic work rather than weaving, when viewed from a short distance (see figure 9).

Tapestries of Peru

Among the many beautiful textile remains which have been found in graves along the southern coast of Peru are examples of woven tapestry, some of which are thought to date back to the sixth century AD and belong, therefore, to the pre-Inca period. They are of a primitive type and resemble in some ways the Coptic tapestries of Egypt. There were, in fact, a number of characteristics in the cultures of Egypt and Peru which were similar, and the custom of using beautifully woven fabrics in which to wrap the dead before burial was one of these. That both countries had similar climates, which were dry enough to preserve such woven fabrics in the tombs for centuries, has also made it possible for us to have access to many specimens of tapestry from both cultures.

The designs which occur in these early Peruvian tapestries contain numerous motifs apparently derived from the mythology of the country, some being representations of a feline divinity, and others of birds such as the eagle and the condor. Fish are also often depicted, but plant motifs are comparatively rare. All of these motifs have an angular form and are very conventionalised. They are used almost exclusively in repetitive patterns, and in this respect early Peruvian tapestries show a close resemblance to Kilim rugs and cannot be said to exploit to the full the flexibility of tapestry technique.

In the later Middle Ages, after the Inca invasion but before the arrival of the Spaniards, the designs of the Peruvian tapestries, which had survived, show a further rather extreme development associated with the conventionalising of motifs: representations of the human head were often simplified by the omission of the mouth, or by merging the nose and mouth into one spot, or even by reducing the human profile to a huge nose; feline motifs were often simplified to the point where only a claw remained. A somewhat similar development is also apparent in Coptic tapestries belonging to the period when the Copts moved away from external influence and worked in the isolation of their monastic institutions.

Following the Spanish invasion in the sixteenth century Inca

weavers came under the influence of Western European tapestry weaving and produced work in which their native art became closely intermingled with that of Spain.

The primitive Peruvian tapestries are thought to have been woven on a type of loom which is still used today in that country, as it is in other parts of South and Central America: this is the backstrap loom, which gets its name from the fact that a belt or band of tape affixed to one end of the loom was passed around the lower back of the weaver. The loom itself consisted of two parallel wooden rods with the warps stretched between them. The warps were not, however, attached directly to the rods, but were passed over small cords running parallel to the rods and attached to them at intervals. The warp yarn passed from one of the cords to the other in a regular lacing or wrapping movement. The tension was obtained in the warps by attaching one of the wooden rods by means of a cord either to a post or the branch of a tree, or to a hook or a beam in a house, whilst the belt or band, which was attached to the other rod, was placed around the lower back of the weaver, who could then easily control the tension by moving his body backwards or forwards as he sat weaving.

Medieval tapestries of Western Europe

It has been thought possible that tapestry weaving could first have come to Western Europe in medieval times through the artisans of Moslem Spain. When Egypt had been invaded by the Arabs, the Coptic tradition of tapestry weaving had been preserved, and the Arab weavers had simply taken it over. As the Moslem invasion spread on through North Africa and into the Iberian Peninsula, the knowledge and the skills which had been acquired from the Coptic weavers in Egypt were carried into other lands, until finally they were established in France and Flanders, where the great efflorescence of Gothic tapestry weaving occurred in the later Middle Ages. One authority even cites the legend that, after Charles Martel had stemmed the tide of the Moorish invasion of Europe in the great battle which took place between Tours and Poitiers in AD 732, some of the conquered Moors who remained in the district settled down to practise and teach the art of tapestry weaving, which since then has been continuously carried on. Evidence which would appear to support this supposition that the tradition of tapestry weaving had been passed on from the Copts of Egypt to the weavers of Western Europe through the Moors of Spain is also seen in the name often given in France and Flanders in medieval times to woven hangings or coverings: they were called *tapis sarrasinois*

11 Circular panel showing emperor with Persian captives, seventh century. Coptic *Victoria and Albert Museum*

and *sarrasinoys werker*. In Germany too, especially on the Upper Rhine, the name for such work was *heidnisch Werk* (heathen work), which indicated that it came from the Moslem world, where lived the great heathen enemies of medieval Christendom.

Some authorities, however, are not convinced that all Western tapestry was derived from the work of the Spanish Moslem weavers. They point to certain of the earliest extant pieces of tapestry weaving to be found in Europe—three fragments, which were originally in the church of St Gereon in Cologne, and are now deposited as follows: one in the museum at Lyons, one in Nuremberg and one in the Victoria and Albert Museum in London. These fragments are thought to have been woven in Germany possibly in the latter half of the eleventh or at the beginning of the twelfth century, and to show the definite influence of Byzantine silk damasks. From this evidence it could be argued that the inspiration to Western European weavers, which led finally to the production of the great medieval tapestries, had come from the East by way of the crusades.

A third suggestion is that the Western European tradition of tapestry weaving, at least as far as Arras is concerned, may go back to the days of the Roman occupation, and in this connection Pliny's reference to the weavers of Gaul as serious rivals to the weavers of Babylon and Alexandria has been quoted in association especially with Arras, as the Atrebates, who lived in that part of Gaul, were most famous as weavers.

However the inspiration to produce tapestry may have come into Europe, there is no doubt as to the magnitude and magnificence of the final achievement. There was in medieval Europe such a great variety of uses to which woven tapestry might be put. Woven woollen hangings were popular, not only for their decorative effect, but also because they added to the comfort of a room and could help resist the cold seeping in from the stone walls of a castle. Rich nobles took their tapestries with them when they travelled, using them to decorate and to help warm the house where they stayed. Generals took them when they went to war in order to line their tents. Hangings were also used to decorate the dais and the stands at a tournament or pageant, and were even hung in the streets from the balconies of houses as decoration when kings or other great persons visited a city. Tapestries could also be used, like curtains, to divide up a great hall. In church they could be used as altar hangings *(antependia)* or, as was especially the case in Germany, when woven in long, narrow strips, they were often used to decorate the backs of pews. This latter practice was similar to one often seen in the houses of well-to-do people in Germany and in what is today

12 Part of a garment from a tomb at El A'zam in Egypt, tenth to twelfth centuries. This beautiful example of later Egyptian weaving is tapestry in silk on a linen warp. It shows definite Islamic influence in design, but retains some slight Coptic naturalistic elements. The outline of the design and the Arabic inscription are woven in red silk on a natural-coloured background. *Victoria and Albert Museum*

13 Detail from a medieval tapestry *Hunting the Wild Birds,* one of a series of hunting tapestries, formerly owned by the Duke of Devonshire, late fifteenth century. This small detail shows the clever use of slits in the face and collar of the falconer, and the simple but exceedingly effective treatment of the falcons. *Victoria and Albert Museum* ▶

called Switzerland, where such long, narrow panels of woven tapestry were fixed along a wall behind a long bench-type seat so that the clothes of persons using the seat were protected against the whitewashed wall.

The earliest known tapestries of Western Europe, which include not only the German St Gereon fragments from Cologne, but also the group of so-called German–Romanesque tapestries, the most important of which are those preserved in the cathedral of Halberstadt in East Germany, show, as do the Coptic tapestries, what has been designated as the *primitive* style. They reveal as yet little evidence of the use of *hachure* in shading from one colour or tone into another, or of the use of slits to suggest the form of an object. Shapes in the design are rendered in blocks of flat colour in a way rather reminiscent of the technique of stained glass, and the design itself is often closely related to the illustrations in illuminated manuscripts. A typical example of this style of tapestry is the panel in the cathedral of Halberstadt which depicts Charlemagne and the four philosophers.

Not until the fourteenth century did the first of what have been called *perfected* tapestries appear in France, worked upon high-warp looms in either Arras or Paris. It was from this time onwards that tapestry first became the most prized form of art amongst kings and nobles in Western Europe: damasks, embroideries and paintings, which had formerly been more highly valued, were now thrown far into the background by the wonderful new tapestries. The development of weaving techniques now became even more important than the development of design, and it was this great advance in technique which distinguished the *perfected* so much from the *primitive* tapestries and made them such remarkable works of art. By exploiting tapestry technique to the full the weaver now discovered how to delineate, for example, elements of the human form in a manner never before achieved in this medium: a bold and effective use of slits, and especially of stepped slits, rendered the form of the face without recourse to frequent changes of colour, as a shadow could be suggested simply by the introduction of a slit or slits—definite, and in this case quite intentional, turn-backs along a warp thread—and the bone-structure of the hand was likewise clearly suggested (see figure 13). This device was also used to show light and shade in human hair or animals' fur and to give depth to the foliage of trees.

This sophisticated use of effects which result purely from elements in the technique of tapestry weaving contrasts strongly with what is seen in primitive tapestries, where slits generally occur accidentally and merely as the result of the chance meeting of two areas of different colour along a line parallel with the

14 Detail from another of the Devonshire hunting tapestries, late fifteenth century. This tapestry which was probably woven in Tournai or Arras, is a fine example of the perfected style of medieval Gothic tapestries. *Victoria and Albert Museum* ►

warp; they are not the outcome of the weaver's studied efforts to render certain details of the cartoon in the most convincing way.

A striking use of *hachure* to obtain shades of a colour is a further characteristic of perfected tapestries. The weavers were limited in the number of colours and shades of a colour which they might use and they, therefore, obtained intermediary shades by hatching one colour into another much lighter or darker one, and it is these so-called hatchings—great vertical lines or spears of colour—which form such a distinguishing feature of the perfected Gothic tapestries (see figures 13 and 14).

Vertical lines were in any case a dominant feature in all important tapestries of the time, because the warp threads generally ran horizontally across the finished piece of work, the tapestries having been woven mainly from the side, and this fact made it easier for the weaver to work vertical lines rather than horizontal ones. Very noticeable and characteristic of the best Gothic tapestry designs is the skilful way in which vertical lines in flat colour are contrasted with horizontal ribs in round relief caused by the warp. It is quite evident from a study of the tapestries of this, the best period of pictorial tapestry weaving, that the technique of line contrast which they reveal is the one best suited to the medium.

Renaissance and Baroque tapestries

From the beginning of the sixteenth century onwards woven tapestry began to decline from the peak of perfection we have noticed in the Gothic period, and this has often been ascribed to the fact that an attempt was made to adapt the technique of tapestry to suit the designs, which had ceased to be two dimensional and had begun to develop perspective. They were designs which were suited to the technique of painting rather than to that of weaving. A good example of this change in design is seen in the great set of tapestries known as *The Acts of the Apostles,* which was based on cartoons painted by Raphael and which skilfully sought to imitate the technique of the great painter. Despite the skill of the weavers these tapestries are less successful than are the best of the Gothic period and this, I believe, is because their designs, being the work of a great painter, were less easy to handle in tapestry technique and did not exploit to the full the inherent qualities of this particular medium as did the best designs of the earlier period, which appear to have been the work of artists who were fully conversant with the requirements of the tapestry loom and made cartoons especially for it.

In the seventeenth century the decline in tapestry design continued with the appearance of Baroque designs, which have a sculptural quality not well suited to weaving. Areas of heavy shadow, which are typical of Baroque painting, were now woven into tapestries, and this technique of contrasting areas of light and shade replaced the earlier simple use of contrasting lines of colour.

The eighteenth and nineteenth centuries and the modern revival

The eighteenth century saw the final decline of tapestry weaving in France: by the time of the French Revolution tapestry designs had become insipid and flat, lacking all strong contrast, whether of line or colour, and nothing of real value was produced from then until the revival of interest in this craft during the present century.

During the second half of the nineteenth century in England there did occur, however, a great upsurge of interest in tapestry through the efforts of William Morris at Merton Abbey, where he and Burne-Jones and their followers caught something of the spirit of the ancient tapestry designers and weavers of the Gothic period in France.

In modern times various people have striven to revive the art of woven tapestry. At Aubusson under the direction of Madame Cuttoli a very skilful effort was made to bring about such a revival, but the results were disappointing because the weavers were asked to attempt the production in tapestry of exact copies of pictures by such famous painters as Rouault, Léger, Braque, Picasso and Dufy. They even wove representations of the frames as well as of the pictures, and the finest shades and the most subtle transitions of colour were rendered, so that, when new, the tapestries could hardly be distinguished from the real paintings they depicted. This was the ultimate subordination of the weaver's technique to that of the painter, and it cannot be regarded as an acceptable development, but rather as a prostitution of the one art-form to the other. In any case, after the passage of a number of years it has been found that the colours of these tapestries have faded in such a way that the former subtleties of colour gradation, produced by the employment of a wide range of shades, have been lost, and this attempt at a revival of tapestry has had to relinquish its one claim to recognition, its slavishly exact imitation of famous paintings.

The painter, Jean Lurçat, has made a much more worthwhile attempt to create a revival of tapestry weaving in modern times, and again this has occurred at Aubusson. His has been a far-reaching experiment to discover what is the possibility of returning to simpler designs which could support his belief in the purely decorative function of tapestry. He has discarded the subtle tone gradations of the Cuttoli school in favour of a mosaic of pure colours—restricted in number—where transitions in colour are made by hatching or stippling one colour with another.

Several other French artists, among them Marcel Gromaire, Jean Picart le Doux and Marc Saint-Saëns, have also played a part in the modern revival of interest in tapestry, and many of them have worked with Jean Lurçat and been influenced by his ideas. A great deal of experimental work is also being carried on in this medium in a number of other countries, and it is to be hoped that this continued interest in a great art-form of the past will produce tapestries of real value which will show a proper appreciation of the true nature of the technique involved.

2 *Designing for woven tapestry*

Special qualities and limitations of the craft

The magnificent examples of the Gothic period in France and Flanders show that tapestry is, at its best, a strong and lively art-form, displaying bold textural qualities which arise from certain elements in its structure. Chief of these is the strong linear contrast created when the lines of colour formed by the weft threads cut across the ribs of the warp, and slits open up across areas of plain colour. It becomes clear from a study of these works of the greatest period of tapestry production that, from its very nature, tapestry is especially suited to the use of designs in which contrasting areas of strong colour are linked together simply by the bold lines of hachure, but it is less successful when used to render subtle colour changes or great intricacy in design.

When, therefore, it is a question of preparing a design for a woven tapestry, it is important first of all to have a proper realisation of how certain elements inherent in the craft place limitations on what can be done but, if properly exploited, can lead to most satisfying results. The first point to realise in this connection is that the direction of the warp in the finished piece of work will have a definite influence upon the nature of the design it is possible to weave. Although all the finest tapestries of the Gothic period had horizontal warps, it is not obligatory to work a tapestry always with the warps running in this way, and some well-known tapestries, including the one of *Christ in Majesty* in Coventry Cathedral, have the warps running vertically. The essential thing is to suit the direction of the warp to the particular design intended to be woven. If the design is one with a preponderance of vertical lines, then it will be most easily and probably also most suitably woven with the warp threads running horizontally across the surface of the finished work; if there are many horizontal lines in a design, then it will be best woven with the warp running vertically. This avoids the necessity of weaving a large number of lines which follow the length of the warp; something which immediately raises prob-

15 Detail of a tapestry chair seat by *Annie Hambrook*. This is based on a traditional floral design. Textural effects are limited, and all slits have been sewn up

lems for the weaver, as at least two warp threads have to be woven over in forming such a line parallel to the warp direction, unless the attempt is to be made to wrap a single warp thread with the weft. This latter is a difficult operation to perform satisfactorily, as the single wrapped warp thread remains isolated from the rest, with slits along each side of it. A number of such isolated warp threads can even be a source of weakness in the fabric of a large tapestry. Furthermore, the effect produced by wrapping a single thread to represent a straight line in the design is liable to be heavy and clumsy as compared with that which can be created by the fine, thin lines it is possible to weave at right angles to the warp, because these lines can be as thin as a single weft thread.

In spite of this, some rather less sophisticated designs than are generally envisaged in thinking of the perfected medieval tapestries can well be woven with a number of the warp threads wrapped either individually or in groups. Modern wall hangings are not woven as screens to offer protection against the cold draughts and the damp which might percolate into a room, so it

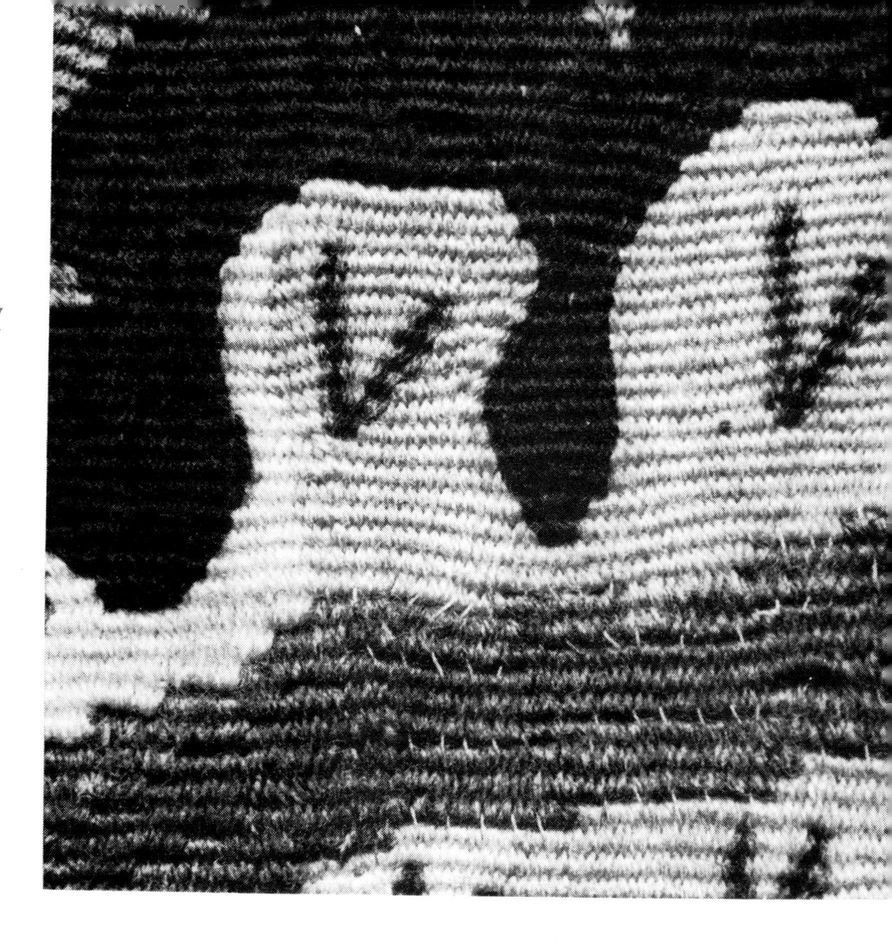

16 Detail of an abstract design, showing how long slits are formed where shallow curves follow the direction of the warp. Where the curves are less shallow, a series of stepped slits is seen. This picture also shows clearly how the ribs formed by the warp tend to stand out in areas of lighter colour but are less visible in darker areas

is of little importance today if even large tapestries are not strong and solid pieces of fabric: they can indeed have numerous long wrapped warp threads hanging detached from one another. Small tapestries can undoubtedly incorporate this feature quite easily. Even in this type of modern design, however, it will certainly be found that the warp direction can still play an important part in establishing the nature of the design which can be woven, and that designs which result in single wrapped warp threads which hang vertically rather than lie horizontally, when the tapestry is placed in position, are the most practical and effective.

Just as straight lines which follow the warp direction can create problems for the weaver, so shallow curves running close to the direction of the warp can also be difficult to weave successfully. Long slits are again liable to be developed, which will need to be stitched up afterwards. All curves, in fact, which approach the direction of the warp, even if they are not particularly shallow, are likely to lead to the development of numerous slits and to a great deal of what is called *stepping* when they are woven.

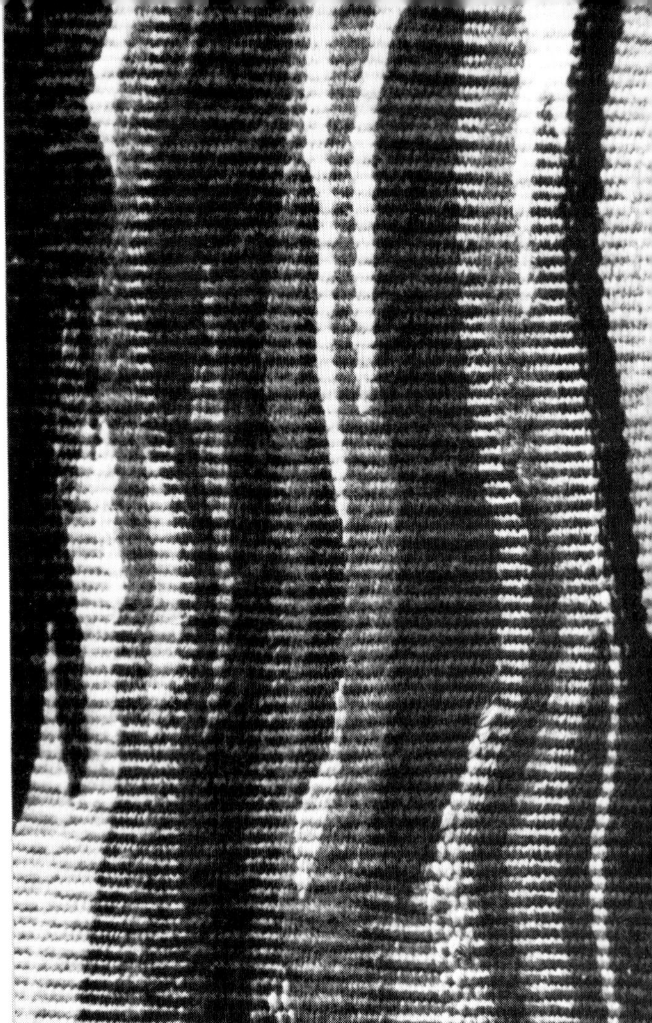

When, however, the designer has acquired a full awareness of the limiting effect which the occurrence of slits in woven tapestry may have upon his work, he should not overlook the fact that they can also offer him great assistance in producing a pleasing design: they are most useful in suggesting relief and in creating the effect of light and shade without having recourse to changes of colour or to the weaving of areas of shadow. They can also be used to add textural interest to modern abstract designs and to provide interesting decorative contrasts in an area woven in one plain colour. In this way slits form perhaps the most interesting element in tapestry texture, and their complete avoidance would lead to the creation of a flat and insipid

17 Detail of a partly-worked tapestry, showing the use of block shading, less suitable for tapestry weaving than is the traditional method of shading by hachure. Block shading is more suited to painting

18 (RIGHT) Detail of *Madonna and Child*. The flowing lines of the weft seen here are a natural feature of woven tapestry

effect. What should be aimed at, therefore, is not designs which seek to avoid the use of slits, but those which reveal a mastery of the correct and effective use of the slit technique.

Another feature of tapestry weaving which is worth bearing in mind, when a suitable design is being sought, is that it is an entirely free type of weaving, where the weft threads seldom run straight across the work from selvedge to selvedge at right angles to the warp, and where individual shapes in a colour are built up independently before other areas of weaving on each side are completed. Strictly repetitive patterns tend, therefore, to limit the freer technique of tapestry and are, in fact, better done in ordinary weaving.

19 *Saint Peter* by *Annie Hambrook*. This panel shows very well the bold textural quality of woven tapestry, resulting from the presence of the ribs and slits which are an integral part of the technique

20 Detail of *Blackbirds in the Garden*, showing the strong linear contrast which occurs in tapestry weaving, when lines of colour formed by the weft cut boldly across the ribs created by the warp

21 A further detail from *Blackbirds in the Garden*

22 An exercise in weaving horizontal lines in alternate colours across the full width of the warp. Weaving begins with a section in which a single pass of each colour is worked. This is followed by sections in which the number of passes of the individual colours is doubled each time a new section begins

In spite of the fact that it is necessary to be acquainted with the technique of tapestry weaving before a successful attempt can be made to design for it, there is no need to feel that this is a difficult craft to master. After weaving a few small pieces—they need not be larger than about 152 mm (6 in.) square—it should be possible to acquire a sufficient knowledge of the technique and of how certain effects can be achieved in tapestry to begin preparing designs with a reasonable chance of success (see figures 22–30). From this point onwards the fewer rules that are laid down for designing the better. Experimentation with new ideas, which is now the order of the day, is, therefore, a thing to be encouraged. I do feel, however, that such experiments in designing for tapestry are best confined to the production of simple, uncomplicated designs with a restricted colour scheme, and with no attempt at the imitation of effects which are especially suited to other media such as painting.

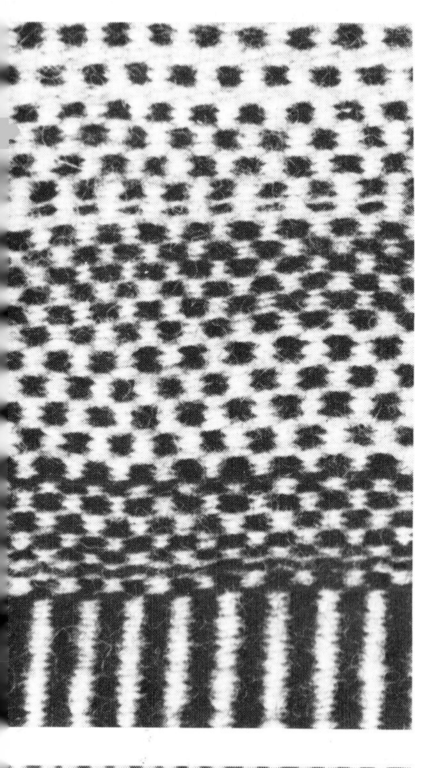

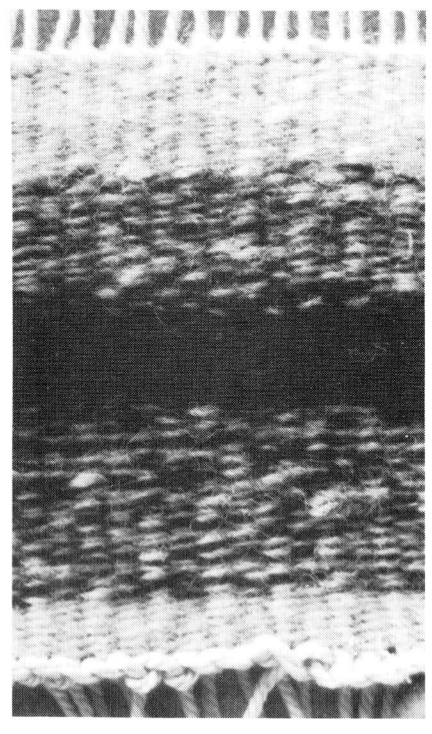

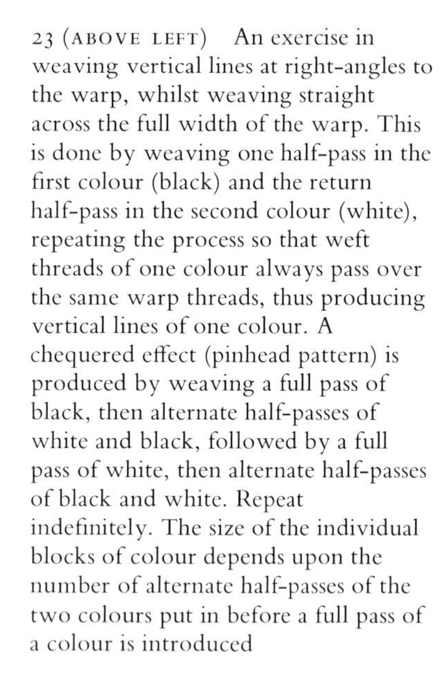

23 (ABOVE LEFT) An exercise in weaving vertical lines at right-angles to the warp, whilst weaving straight across the full width of the warp. This is done by weaving one half-pass in the first colour (black) and the return half-pass in the second colour (white), repeating the process so that weft threads of one colour always pass over the same warp threads, thus producing vertical lines of one colour. A chequered effect (pinhead pattern) is produced by weaving a full pass of black, then alternate half-passes of white and black, followed by a full pass of white, then alternate half-passes of black and white. Repeat indefinitely. The size of the individual blocks of colour depends upon the number of alternate half-passes of the two colours put in before a full pass of a colour is introduced

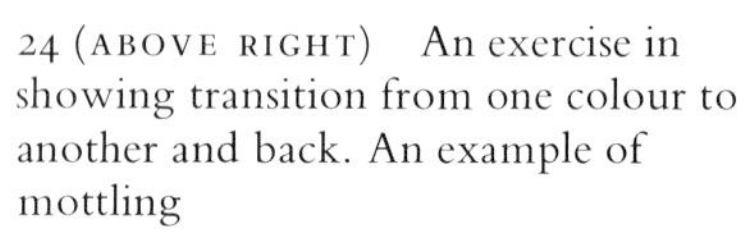

24 (ABOVE RIGHT) An exercise in showing transition from one colour to another and back. An example of mottling

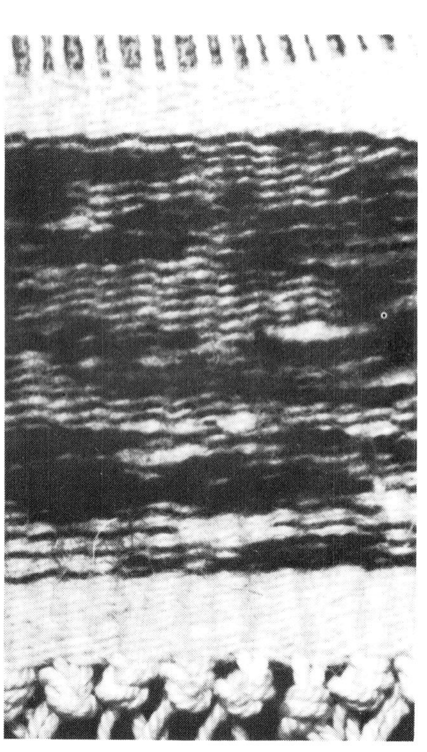

25 (BELOW LEFT) Line hatchings worked as an exercise. These are short passes of irregular length against a contrasting background. On the reverse side, loops of weft thread are left floating and form an interesting textural effect

26 (BELOW RIGHT) Reverse side of the exercise in line hatchings, showing floating threads of weft

27 (ABOVE LEFT) Close-up specimen of line hatchings

28 (ABOVE RIGHT) An exercise in the working of various forms of hachure

29 (BELOW LEFT) An example of free tapestry weaving, demonstrating the use of *crapaud* or *ressort,* a device often employed by Coptic weavers, to pick out a pattern or show the form of a figure. The line of the *crapaud* leaps freely from place to place and has sometimes been mistaken for superimposed embroidery

30 (BELOW RIGHT) An exercise in working a simple counter-change pattern

Modern freely-woven tapestries

Freedom of design is, of course, limited to an extent by the purpose for which the finished piece of work is intended. In designing for a picture or wall hanging it is possible to adopt a very much freer treatment of the subject than in designing for a furniture covering. When weaving tapestry for the latter purpose, there are limitations in so far as experimentation in design goes, but certain textural effects can be aimed at in order to enliven a design. When designing for a wall hanging, it is possible to contemplate such things as leaving some of the warps bare; varying the thickness of the weft; mixing tapestry weave with ordinary tabby weave; threading on beads or other forms of embellishment; adding extra warps through the slits in the tapestry and building up three-dimensional effects. These ideas need thinking about carefully before the design is made,

31 (LEFT) An unfinished example of modern, freely-woven tapestry in which threads were tied to the frame at random and used as warp. Extra threads were added where necessary as the weaving proceeded. Natural-coloured twine and black thread were used as warp, with wool, silk and cotton in shades of blue, green and gold, together with a certain amount of gold lurex, for the weft

32 (RIGHT) Detail of 31

33 (LEFT) Detail of a tapestry woven in strips and joined at intervals with extra threads

34 (RIGHT) Detail of a freely-woven piece, showing the use of raised chain band, generally considered an embroidery stitch. As this stitch has to be worked on transverse threads, it is in the author's opinion a natural choice for working on warps and is, therefore, as much a weaving method as is *soumak*

but the main thing to do, when working on articles of this kind, is to enjoy oneself and not be afraid of trying out new ideas.

When designs are produced in this way, forms of weaving can be arrived at rather far from the traditional woven tapestry, and there are to be seen today many types of woven wall hangings and three-dimensional hanging objects, sometimes known as woven sculpture which, although they may be classed as tapestry, have little real relationship to the perfected tapestries of the past. They have arisen through experimentation in the use of unusual materials in weaving and through a combination of traditional tapestry techniques with elements from the more primitive weaving of earlier days among remote peoples, together with other elements from related forms of free-weaving of a modern, sophisticated type.

35 A dried thistle head can suggest a tapestry design with exciting lines

Sources of designs

People often ask me, where exactly ideas for tapestry designs can be found. My reply is that ideas for suitable designs are everywhere—around us at all times simply awaiting discovery. We do, however, need to look carefully and not just superficially at the objects among which we live in order to discover in them shapes and lines which are attractive and which can inspire us to produce the design we seek. Even a pile of cups and saucers, or a collection of cutlery, or a stack of chairs can offer an interesting idea for a design, if we are able to comprehend it.

Nature has, of course, always been the chief source of inspiration to the designer, who can readily discover beautiful curves and pleasing shapes in flowers and plants of all descriptions. Their colours and textures may also help him to break up sections of a design and to add further interest to it. Such an ordinary natural object as a vegetable marrow can provide a

36 A greatly magnified photograph of a seed-head from a tassel hyacinth with its shadow, could be an inspiration for a design

useful exercise in this latter respect, if, for instance, we observe the lines of colour and the stippling effects upon its surface, and then try to interpret into tapestry weave whatever is there revealed to us. Other sources of inspiration exist in such things as coral and seaweed, birds and fishes, and the colourful wings of butterflies, whilst much can be gained by observing the shapes formed by the intersections of branches and twigs against the sky, by clouds and by reflections of all kinds.

It is often a good idea to begin one's search for a suitable design from a chosen natural object by making a sketch of it, however rough, as this helps to reveal details in the subject under consideration which might not have been clearly noticed in a more superficial study. A sketch is also useful to keep for later reference, if one is not ready to start weaving the design immediately. I suggest, however, that such a sketch, whilst being made as accurate a reproduction of the original object as possible, should not be used just as it is to supply a design from which to weave a realistic representation of nature. Any object from which a design is to be drawn should, I think, be treated simply as a starting point: it should merely provide the spark which sets off the process of thought by which some original arrangement of elements from nature may be discovered and then developed into the required design. I feel, therefore, that it is best to select only a part of an original sketch and to enlarge that. On the enlarged drawing it is a good idea to experiment with the shapes which have appeared, endeavouring to find the rhythm which runs through them, as through all natural things, and hoping thus to discover a pleasing line by which all the existing shapes may be connected and unified into a satisfactory design.

Another method which I have used to obtain interesting designs direct from nature is to cut cross-sections of fruits, vegetables or the seed-heads of flowering plants, or to take other suitable pieces of natural material, and to observe them under a powerful magnifying glass, or to place small, thin sections of them between glass so as to make a slide which can be projected upon a screen. A photograph may then be taken of the projected image, and from this an exciting design may result, which will be excellent for tapestry.

Apart from purely natural objects, man-made things such as buildings, especially blocks of high-rise flats and offices, scaffolding, pylons, cranes, timber yards, docks, parts of ships and watches, architectural, industrial and scientific drawings, photographs of machinery in newspapers and magazines and scores of other everyday things can provide the inspiration needed to produce a design which will be suitable for tapestry weaving.

37 (OPPOSITE ABOVE LEFT) The flower of the magnolia *grandiflora* offers beautifully curved shapes for a possible tapestry design

38 (OPPOSITE ABOVE RIGHT) A close-up detail of a magnolia flower just opening, which could well be developed into a suitable design

39 (OPPOSITE BELOW LEFT) A further detail of the magnolia

40 (OPPOSITE BELOW RIGHT) The graceful lines of seed-heads and twigs on a tree in the Agora at Athens could provide inspiration for a delicate, yet lively design

Helpful inspiration to the tapestry designer can also result from a visit to a museum, where so many beautiful and interesting objects of all kinds may be studied. At the Victoria and Albert Museum in London one can, of course, spend a long time in the quiet, secluded rooms, where some of the finest examples of the wonderful Gothic tapestries of the fifteenth and sixteenth centuries are kept, contemplating how well the designers and weavers of that golden age of tapestry suited their designs to the medium. We must not, however, allow ourselves to become discouraged by the magnificence of these pieces into feeling that we today cannot hope to produce worthwhile woven tapestries. These fine examples of the craft reveal a true image of their age; they were executed by many expert weavers, working from dawn to sunset over a number of years in a style which was perfectly suited to their times. It is possible that modern tapestry weavers may, in the present revival of interest in their craft, be inspired to the attainment of another golden age, which will be something quite different from what has been seen before, but will also be a true reflection of its day and age.

Yet another way of proceeding to find a design, and one which is particularly useful to those who have difficulty in drawing, is the cut-paper method: simple shapes are cut out of paper and then arranged to form a pleasing design. If thin tissue paper is used for this purpose and some of the shapes are overlapped, new shapes can be created where the original ones show through one another, and this helps to develop the original concept further. The main consideration at this stage is not to allow the design to become too complicated, so the development of additional shapes must not be allowed to proceed too far. This is in itself a useful exercise in training oneself to be selective in assembling shapes to form a design.

As soon as a satisfactory result has been achieved from the cut-paper arrangement, place a piece of tracing-paper over the whole and trace the outline of the shapes through. If it is then felt necessary, further details, such as connecting lines between shapes or perhaps some extra shapes, can be added. It is worth remembering that, although simple designs are usually the most effective, too much plain background should be avoided in the final design.

41 (OPPOSITE ABOVE LEFT) A silver-grey leaf found upon the ground in Athens yields an interesting motif for a design

42 (OPPOSITE ABOVE RIGHT) A dried-up rose cutting from the garden which could lead to a suitable design

43 (OPPOSITE BELOW LEFT) This weathered piece of stone from a distant beach suggests shapes which could well be woven

44 (OPPOSITE BELOW RIGHT) A section of a melon is another possible source for a design

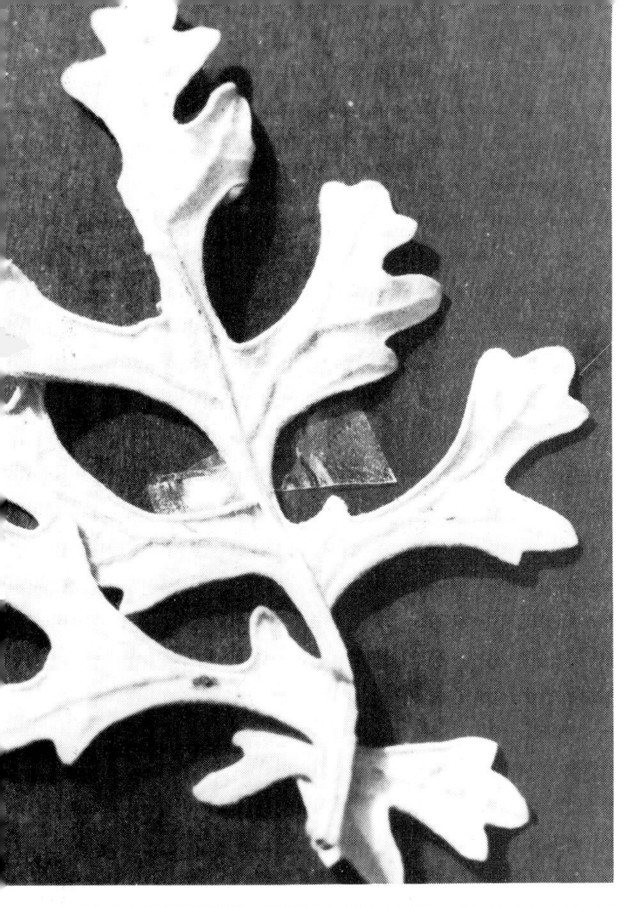

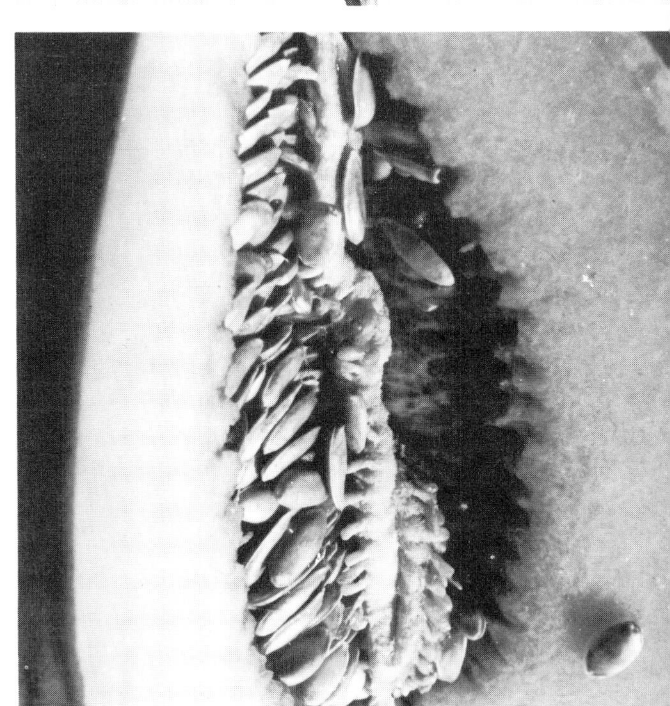

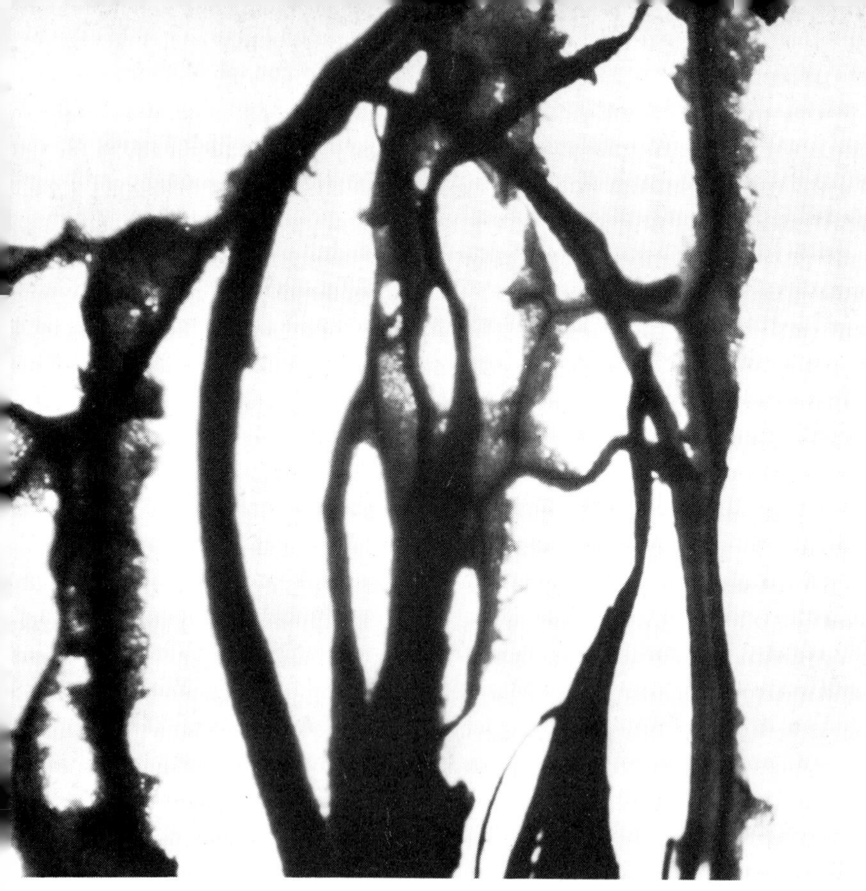

45 A design revealed when a section of orange pith was sandwiched between glass to make a slide, then projected onto a screen

46 The projected image of a slide containing grasses

Drawing up the final design

A tapestry could well be started without first having a definite fixed design to work from, by the weaver's drawing inspiration simply from the materials being used and thus arriving at a satisfactory abstract design as the weaving progresses, but most people will probably need to work from a prepared design. This should be drawn up to the full size intended for the finished work and should either be painted in the desired colours or have some indication of the colour scheme incorporated in it by a system of numbering the different shades of wool and entering these numbers in the appropriate places on the design. All the shapes used in this final design must form a unified and well-balanced whole, and careful consideration should be given to the nature of the shapes which will remain as areas of background, when the design is woven. It is often helpful before making the final working drawing to paint in just these background shapes upon a separate sheet of paper, in order to discover whether they form just as pleasing and well balanced an image as do the superimposed design shapes. One should also check that the design possesses a satisfactory centre of interest, which will draw and hold the attention of the viewer. This can take the form of an exciting area of colour or an arresting shape or group of shapes. The centre of interest must, however, be harmonised with the whole of the design as, whatever the nature of the piece of work concerned, it must appear to be a single entity. The boundaries of the various zones of colour must be clearly outlined and, when it is desired to shade from one colour into another, this should be indicated on the design by hatching the area involved with lines, which will be rendered in the weaving by means of the usual spike-shaped hatchings. The places where it is intended that slits should occur should also be indicated on the design.

Some people prefer, when producing a design, to make their original drawing quite small, and by this means they often gain confidence. This small drawing then has to be enlarged up to the size of the piece of work contemplated. A very accurate way of doing this is by the method of squaring-up: the surface of the small drawing is covered with a grid of small squares, while the larger paper to be used for making the enlargement is also squared up with a grid containing the same number of larger squares. The squares are numbered on both the small drawing and the large paper, and by their aid the original drawing is then easily drawn-up in an enlarged form on the larger paper. Another method of enlarging a small design, which is quick but not quite so accurate, is to take a small black and

47 (ABOVE) Tapestry detail. The design was based on an illustration in a science magazine

48 (LEFT) Modern buildings with their soaring lines are an inspiration to those seeking an interesting, modern design

white sketch, photograph it and enlarge the photograph to the size required. The resultant picture will generally need some corrections, but this can be a helpful method for anyone who cannot draw well. When the weaving is to be done on a small frame, this enlarged photograph can be pinned or otherwise fixed behind the warp and used as the working drawing or, if it is preferred, a tracing can be taken from the enlarged photograph for this purpose.

Generally the original full-sized design is traced upon either tracing-paper or tracing-linen, and this tracing becomes the working drawing which is attached behind the warp. These tracings are usually done in black on white, either with black paint or with a felt-tipped pen, so that they can easily be seen through the warp threads, when weaving is taking place. The original coloured drawing can then be used as a guide to the weaver for colour. One point it is necessary to remember at this stage, however, is that, when such a tracing is fixed behind the warp and used as the working drawing, the design will be reversed in the course of the weaving, as the latter is almost always done from the back of the work. If it is important to avoid reversing the design in this way, one has merely to reverse the tracing before attaching it to the back of the warp, something which is easily done when tracing-paper or tracing-linen has been used.

When the actual weaving begins, an initial 12 mm ($\frac{1}{2}$ in.) of plain weaving, which forms a selvedge, is put in to enable the warp threads to be evenly spaced, and the paper design can be fixed in position by pinning one edge of it at intervals along the length of this selvedge. The other edge of the design can be held in position by placing a narrow, flat, wooden bar under both it and the warp with its ends resting on the side bars of the weaving frame and by pinning the edge of the design to it with drawing pins. A piece of string tied across in a similar position from one side bar of the frame to the other may be sufficient, instead of the wooden bar, to hold the paper design in place, but it will then be necessary to watch that the design does not get out of position during the weaving.

3 *Texture and colour*

The principal textural effects in woven tapestry are caused by the occurrence of ribs in the surface when the warp threads are covered by the weft. These effects vary according to the direction of the ribs in the finished panel and also according to whether they are crossing areas of light or dark colour: the ribbed effect becomes much more noticeable on light areas and tends to be obscured on dark ones. Hatchings, which are lines or spires of colour used for shading from a light colour into a darker one, or vice versa, create middle tones. They usually cut across the ribs of the warp at right angles and so form a strong contrast of flat colour against their round relief. As the ribbed effect of the warp is somewhat obscured in the area of the darker hatchings, it is made more noticeable in the areas of high light, which appear in consequence to come forward in the picture. The combined effect of these contrasts created in the perfected medieval tapestries a remarkable illusion of great depth of form and richness of texture.

49 (OPPOSITE ABOVE LEFT) Detail showing the textural effect of hatchings cutting across the ribs formed by the warp

50 (OPPOSITE ABOVE RIGHT) Further detail showing textural effect of hatchings against ribs

51 (OPPOSITE BELOW LEFT) This detail shows how ribs tend to be less apparent on areas of dark colour

52 (OPPOSITE BELOW RIGHT) A good example of tapestry texture is seen in this detail from *Fighting Cocks*

Textural effects are also produced in tapestry by the use of slits. A slit is a turn-back in the weaving, either caused accidentally where two areas of different colour coincide along the line of a warp, or created intentionally by the weaver. Accidental slits generally need to be stitched up carefully after the weaving is completed, but intentional slits are an important part of the design and are left unstitched. They are used to suggest shadows and can also help to break up an uninteresting plain surface. When the human figure occurs in a design for tapestry, slits are of great importance in the modelling of flesh and in indicating the structure of bones and muscles. They are also useful where a slight, but definite line is needed in a place where a change of colour or an outline in colour might appear too hard or heavy. The exact effect of this simple process of breaking up an area of flat colour by means of slits is difficult to define, but it is surprisingly lively and causes the whole slitted area to stand out and to gain in interest.

53 (OPPOSITE ABOVE LEFT) The combined effect of hatchings, slits and ribs is illustrated in this detail

54 (OPPOSITE ABOVE RIGHT) This piece of work shows the decorative effect obtained on a plain-coloured ground by the use of diagonal slits and wrapped warp threads

55 (OPPOSITE BELOW LEFT) A panel with a geometric design, where increased textural effects have been obtained by placing additional warp threads through slits and then weaving over them

56 (OPPOSITE BELOW RIGHT) Part of a tapestry showing extra warp threads taken through slits and woven over. In this way, added interest was given to an abstract design.

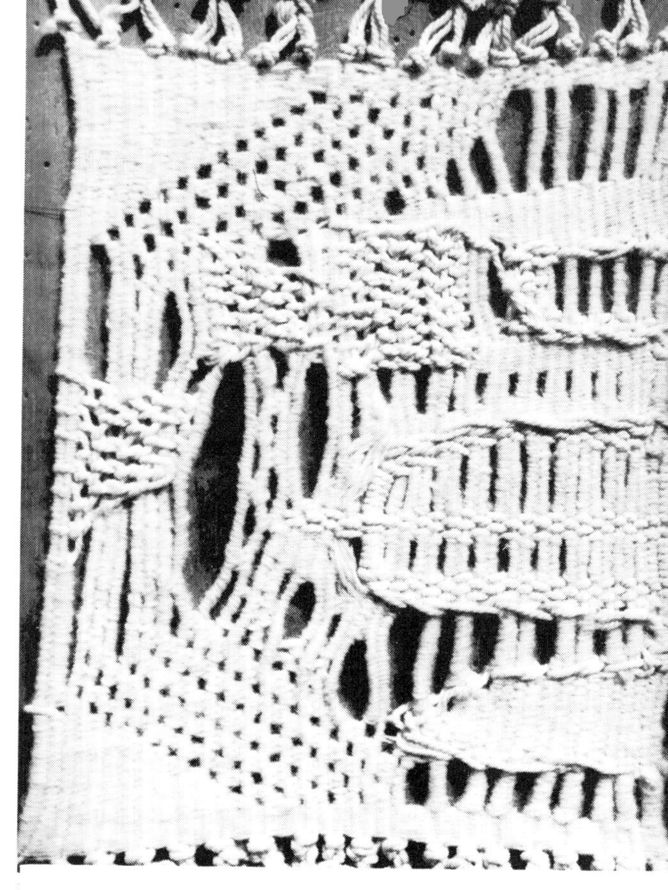

Although slits will not have the same impressive effect, when used in the weaving of small tapestries, as is obtained in large hangings, where the great weight of the tapestry causes the slits to open up and become pronounced, they will nevertheless be quite clearly visible, if the finished panel is fixed upon a stretcher before framing, and they can still give greatly increased life and interest to the work.

Other textural effects can be created in woven tapestry by the employment of a variety of weft materials. Normally in the past tapestries were woven mainly in wool with some silk and perhaps occasionally gold and silver thread. Today a greater variety of materials can be used, and a skilful combination of contrasting weft materials can enable a weaver to heighten the naturally strong textural contrasts of ribs, hatchings and slits. Besides a great variety of man-made and natural fibres, such things as grasses, stalks of dried plants and flowers and twigs can today be woven into tapestries, and beads and similar embellishments can also be used, threading them on to the weft thread and weaving them into the tapestry so that they are visible upon the surface.

57 A small panel with gold, white and cream threads of varying thicknesses, used as weft. Also, extra threads of thin rayon used as warp, superimposed and radiating from a central pearl bead. The extra warp threads have been woven over in places with rayon and lurex thread. *Winnie Browning*

58 A close-up of the central portion of figure 57, showing how the extra warp threads were attached to the pearl bead in the centre

59 Part of a freely-woven panel, with dried stalks and sections of plastic mesh used as weft

60 Detail of a panel in which thick and thin nylon thread has been used as weft upon warp of extra fine nylon thread

61 Part of a panel with a warp of fine metal thread and coarse cotton and a weft of gold metal and black threads

62 (OPPOSITE) A freely-woven panel where many warp threads have been left exposed and the weft, of thick cotton thread, has been woven into coiled shapes around a central point. This centre consists of small stones of interesting shapes. They are attached by threads to the warp. Pieces of cellophane and mohair are contained within a frame of thick twine

63 A small panel with coils of thick wool worked on thin cotton warp, the threads of warp being unevenly spaced

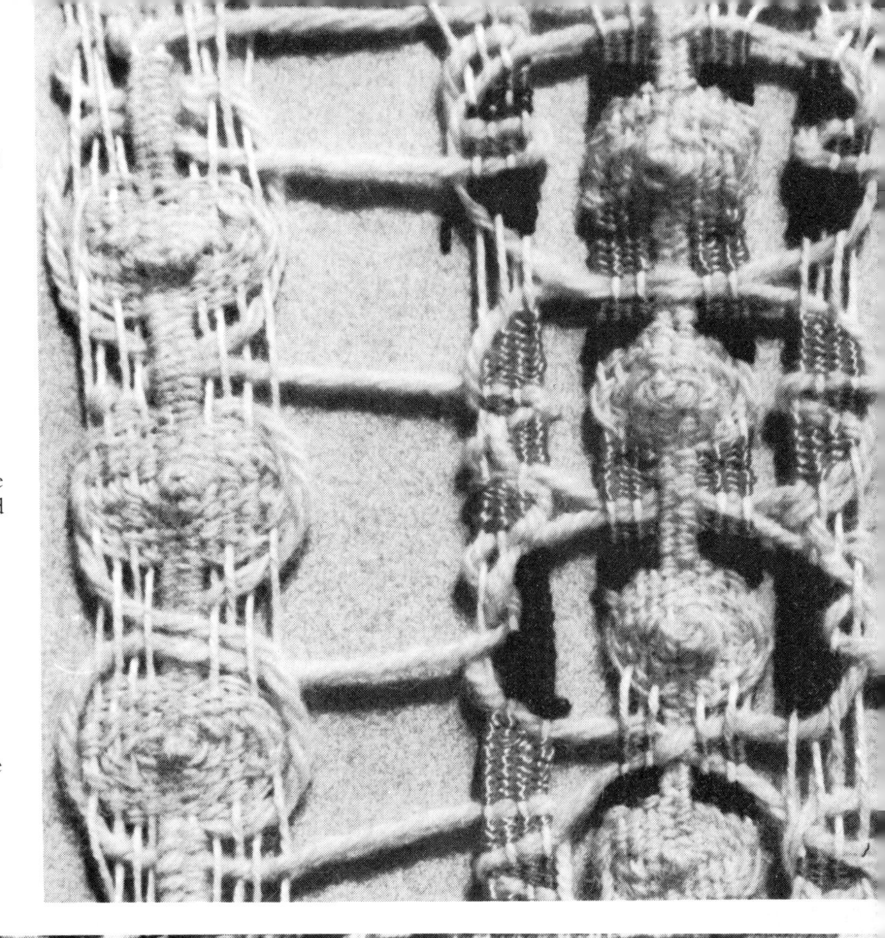

64 (BELOW) This panel shows the use of a variety of weft threads woven upon cotton warp. The latter is only partly covered and has some threads knotted together to give an extra decorative effect

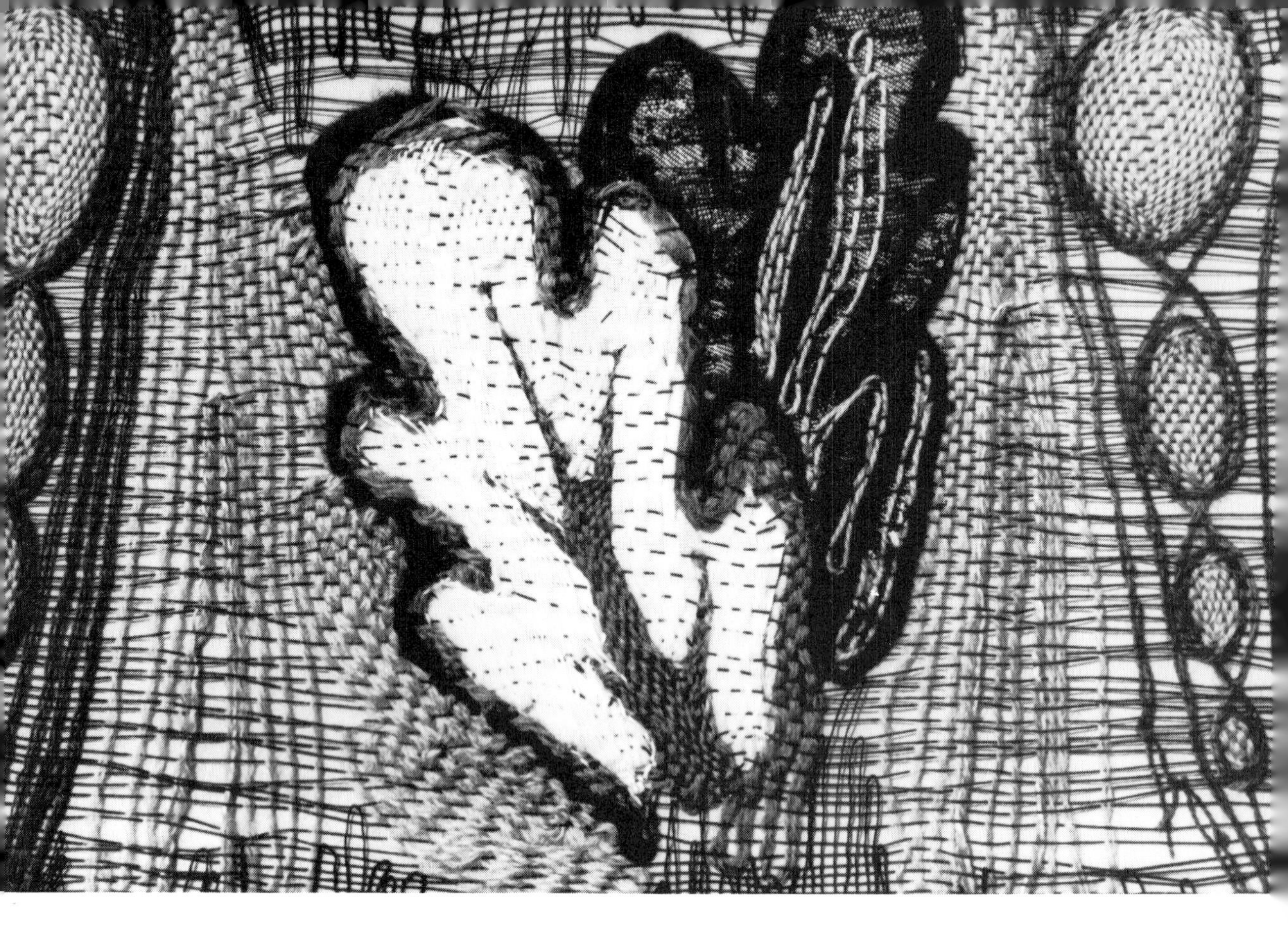

65 Black linen button thread has been used here for warp. The weft consists of some of the same material, plus woollen threads of varying thicknesses

Further textural contrast can be obtained in a tapestry by varying the thickness of the warp and particularly by experimenting with thick weft threads on thin warp, beside thin weft on thick warp. This sort of variation is quite possible to give added interest to furniture coverings as well as to tapestry panels. When in a piece of tapestry intended as furniture covering, however, thin warps are employed between areas of thicker warp, the number of thin warp threads to the inch (cm) should be increased over the number of thick warp threads in order to preserve the same density in the work and to prevent the fabric developing weak patches. If this is done, the areas where thicker warp has been used should then simply appear as slightly raised above the rest of the surface. In a wall panel or hanging areas of extra thin warp can be introduced quite well without increasing the number of warp threads to the inch (cm), and then the areas

66 A panel showing the use of the gauze technique, in which the warp threads are twisted around one another to form an area of open-work between areas of normal tapestry weave

of widely spaced thin warp threads can be used to give additional interest to the work without impairing its practical usefulness.

Other interesting textural effects can be achieved by manipulating the warp: some areas of the warp can be left bare and the individual warp threads can be twisted together to form interlacing patterns. Such areas of bare warp are interspersed between areas of normal tapestry weaving (see figure 66).

The use of a tufted type of weave, such as was sometimes employed in Coptic tapestry weaving, is another method of adding variety to the texture (see figure 67), as is also the employment of a weaving technique whereby the weft thread is not simply carried over and under alternate warp threads, but is sometimes allowed to pass under several warp threads at once during weaving, so that loops of weft are left floating upon the finished surface (see figure 72).

67 The tufted technique, seen in some early Coptic tapestries, is shown here in a small modern piece

68 (BELOW) *Desert City* by *Val Rhodes*. This panel is woven in wool, silk and rayon. It shows formalised Arab buildings in white, black and blue on a broken yellow foreground, against a sky of pink, orange and red. This scene appears through a great Arab archway, worked in various shades of purple wool, silk and rayon. Textural effect is given to the archway by loops of weft thread left floating

69 (OPPOSITE ABOVE LEFT) A good example of the textural effect of ribs, slits and hatchings. It shows clearly how the ribs tend to disappear in dark areas of colour.

70 (OPPOSITE ABOVE RIGHT) A further example of tapestry texture

71 (OPPOSITE BELOW LEFT) A diamond pattern reinforced by diagonal slits

72 (OPPOSITE BELOW RIGHT) Detail of the panel *Tropical Fruit*, showing a section of background where lengths of weft thread have been taken over several warp threads at a time and left floating. This was achieved by working from the front of the work

73 *St Boniface* by *Mary Rhodes*

74 *Man's Head* by *Miriam Bawden*

75 *Woman's Face* by *Miriam Bawden*
Figures 73, 74 and 75 show the use of hatchings and slits to give form to human features

76 *Madonna and Child* by *Winnie Browning*. This panel shows a simple but charming and effective representation of human figures

77 Detail of *Frog* panel. A richly textured effect has been achieved by a skilful application of true tapestry technique

In the Gothic tapestries only a few colours were used. Those immense wall hangings were usually woven in wool with a scheme of colours which consisted of three or four shades in each of the following colours: red, green, yellow, blue and grey. Sometimes early examples of tapestry had a colour range of as few as twelve to fifteen shades altogether. The reason why the number of shades could be so limited was that the method of shading one colour into another by means of hachure—lines of one colour striking deep into the adjoining one, dark into medium and medium into light—created the optical illusion of an extra shade between adjacent hatchings, so that three shades of a particular colour could give the illusion of being five.

I think that in modern tapestries we should also limit the number of colours we employ as much as possible, while still retaining three shades of each colour, dark, medium and light, with perhaps an extra very dark shade and one very light coloured silk to give occasional additional depth or brightness to an area of colour.

In choosing a colour scheme for a tapestry it should be remembered that the medium shade in a colour range is the most important one, as it sets the true colour for the whole range. If then it is decided to use red for a certain part of a design, the choice must first be made as to the particular red colour that is required—scarlet, crimson or vermilion. When the exact colour has been chosen, it should be taken as the medium shade of the range, and then a much darker shade and a much lighter shade of the same colour should be chosen to complete the range. A very pale or neutral shade of silk or cotton can be added to the range where highlights are needed. In order to obtain the best effects from this limited range of colours it is necessary to use strong colours with a decided difference between one shade and another.

In addition to the use of hachure to achieve a blending together of colours, such devices as mottling and stippling can also be used. In the former, intermediary shades are obtained by mixing threads of different colours or shades of one colour on the same shuttle or in the same needle. A mottled effect can thus be given to an area of colour, or the mixing of colours can be done in such a way as to give a gradual transition from one colour to another. The transition from black to white, for instance, can be achieved by using the following successive combinations with four strands of fine yarn: start with four black threads together and weave several passes; replace one of these black threads with white and weave a further few passes;

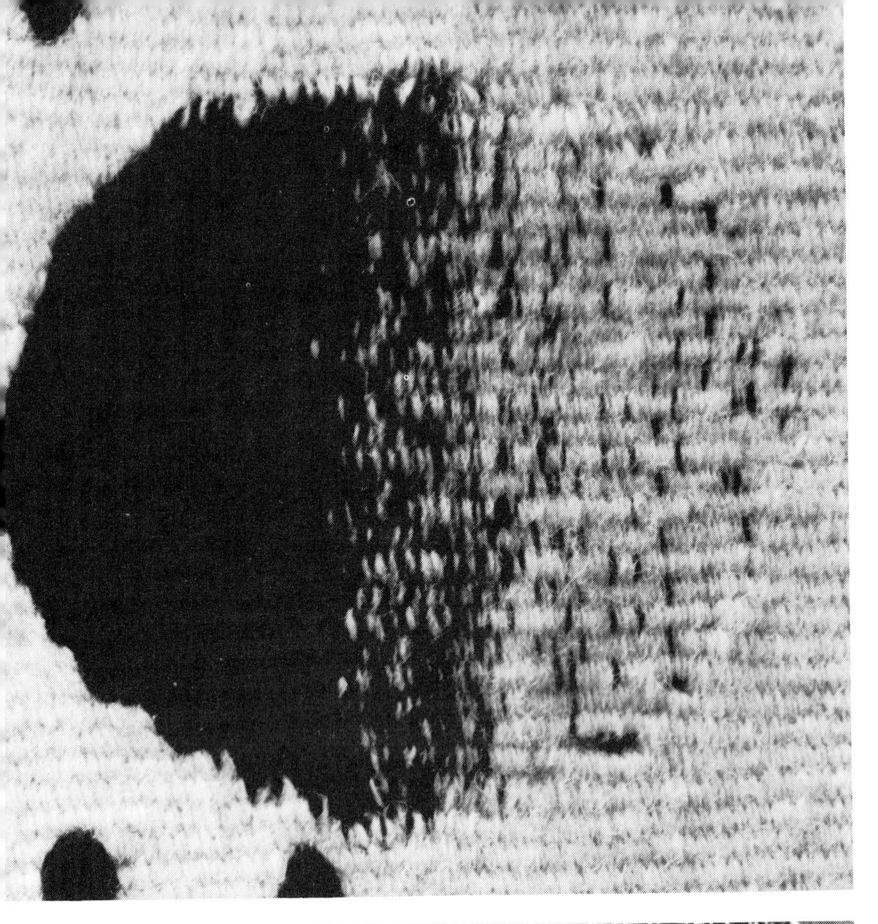

78 An exercise in which gradation of tone is achieved by mottling in the central circular shape, and stippling in the background

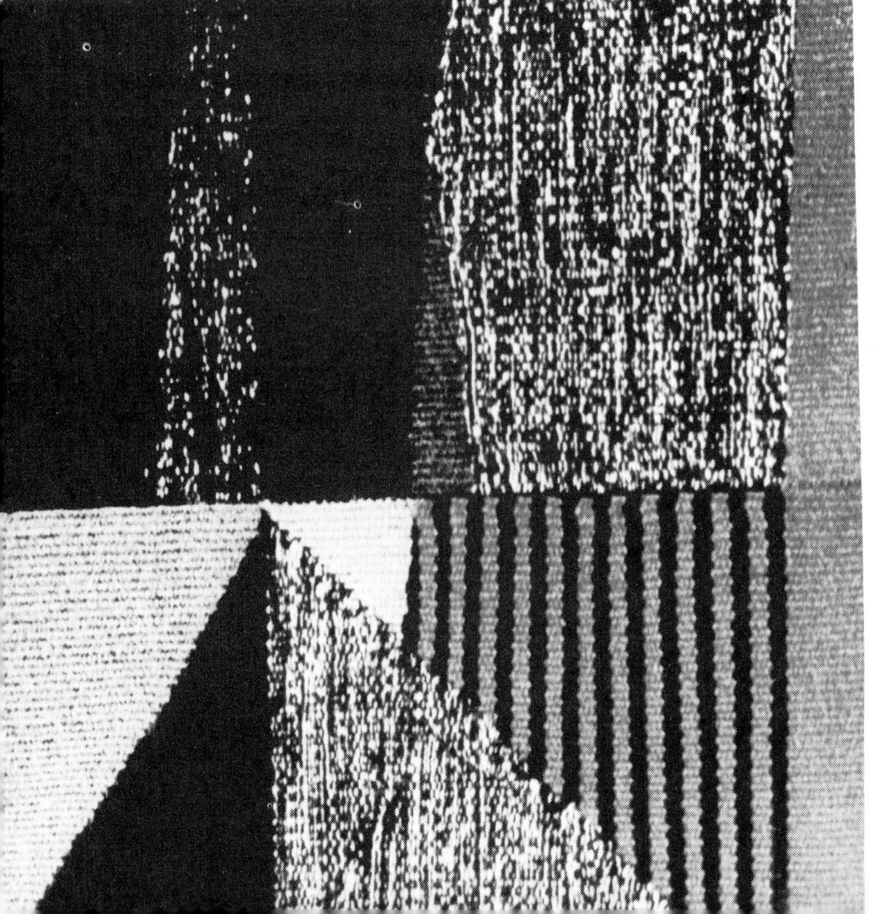

79 A geometric design showing areas of mottling. The two sections of the design have been joined by interlocking the weft as weaving proceeded

80 Stippled effect produced by weaving pin-heads of one colour on a background of another. This was achieved by alternating one half-pass of a colour with three full passes of the other

then weave another area with two threads of black and two of white together; follow this with a similar area woven with one black and three white threads together; and finally work several passes in plain white. The transition from pure black to pure white thus passes through three areas of grey of varying depth of colour. Stippling is the process by which gradations of colour are achieved by weaving spots or flecks of one colour upon a ground of another colour and obtaining intermediate shades by increasing or decreasing the number of flecks or spots in a given area. A combination of hachure with stippling upon areas of pure colour is the method used by the famous French tapestry designer, Jean Lurçat, to obtain intermediary shades and transitions of colour.

81 (LEFT) Linked stippling is here combined with hatchings to achieve gradations of colour

82 (RIGHT) Detail showing the use of stippling in several colours to break up a flat background

When considering the various ways in which colour gradation can be obtained by mixing individual colours together or by placing one colour against another, it is necessary to bear in mind that in tapestry weaving, as in painting, the character of a colour can be changed when it is brought into close proximity with another colour. Green, for example, which is, of course, a mixture of blue and yellow, will appear darker and bluer when placed next to yellow, and lighter and more yellow when next to blue; it will also seem greener against pink than it does against another green tint. A red will appear much more intense next to green than next to any other colour; a pink will look pale next to red, but will become richer if placed beside green, its complementary colour; a neutral grey will appear pinkish next to green and greenish next to red.

The Desert City, as seen through an Arab keyhole archway. Designed and woven by Val Rhodes

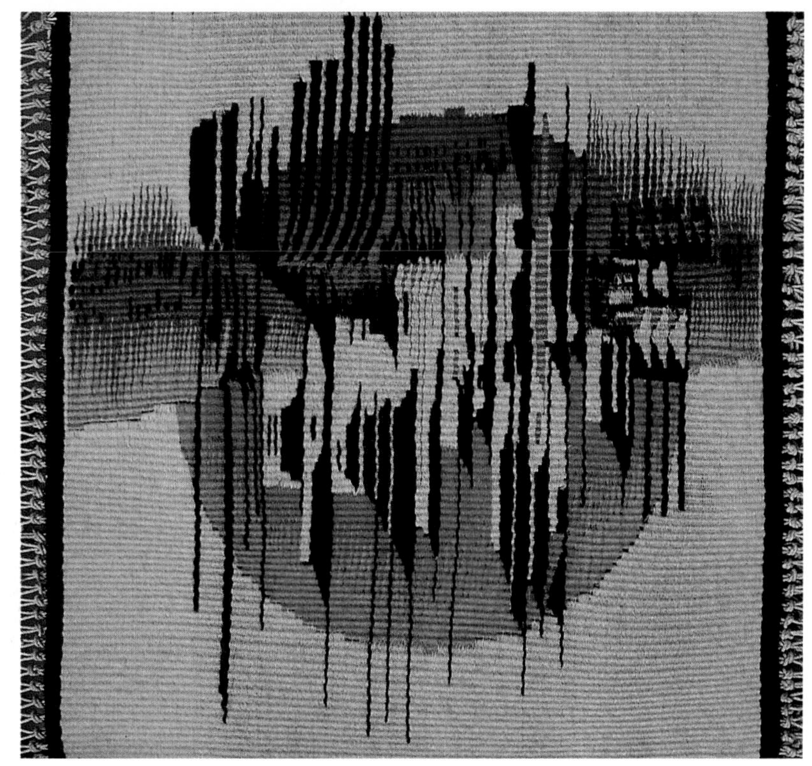

The City in the Sun, designed and woven by Val Rhodes

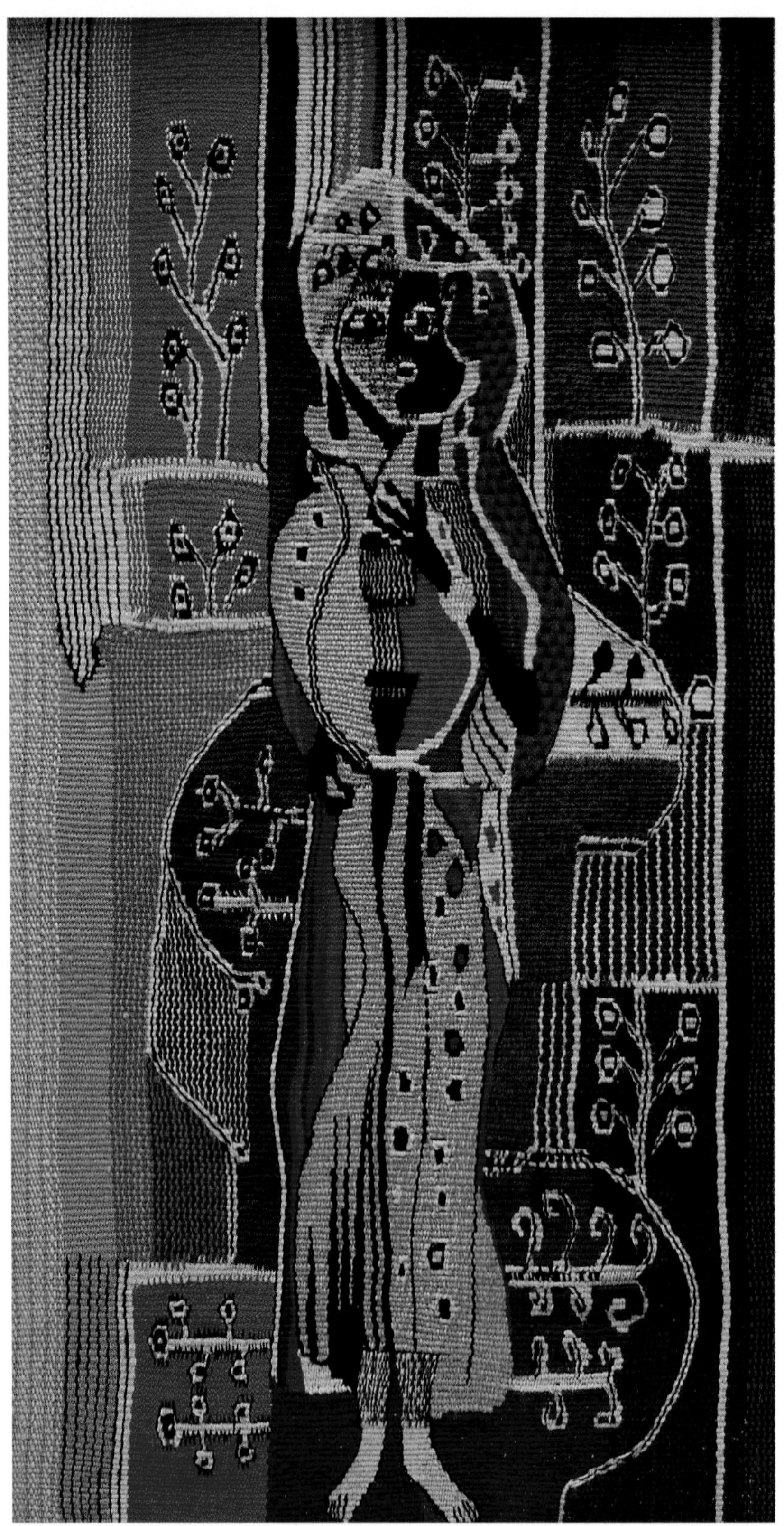

Music, woven by Winnie Browning

Sheep Among Flowers in a Meadow, woven by Miriam Bawden

The Head of Boniface,
woven by the author

The Head of a Horse, woven by the author

Landscape, woven by Lilian Hill

Abstract Panel, woven by Doris Warans

Sprightly Bird, with a heavily textured background, woven by Dorothy Hassock

Opposite: Abstract design for a firescreen, woven by Winnie Browning

Abstract panel, woven with natural dyed wood and lurex by Dorothy Hassock

The finished panel of the illustration on page 138, woven by Winnie Browning

The Dragon Tree, designed and woven by Val Rhodes

The Seated Deer, woven by Miriam Bawden

Butterflies and Foliage, woven by Dorothy Hassock. The design for this tapestry was based on a large panel by Picard le Doux

Panel of large flowers, woven by Winnie Browning

Abstract panel woven by the author

Detail showing a beautifully woven little dog taken from the Lady of the Unicorn set of tapestries

Head of Man, woven by Miriam Bawden

Sky, Mountains and Water, a Scottish scene designed and woven by Margaret Bowden

Landscape. The houses in the foreground are woven on a much finer warp than the rest of the work. Designed and woven by D. Brook

Crested Birds by Lilian Hill. Bold lines and the achievement of textile effects by the clever use of colour are a feature of this panel

Pacahontas by Lilian Hill. This amusing face is freely woven. The ends of the warp threads are wrapped and plaited

83 Another example of stippling, used to give interest to a plain area of background

When mottling is used, and strands of weft in complementary colours of the same tonal value are mixed together, it will be noticed that the effect produced will be that of grey. It is, however, a good idea to obtain the effect of grey in this way rather than to use a plain grey weft material, as the latter can often appear rather dull as compared to the more lively result which will be achieved by mixing bright pinks, blues and yellows together to give the illusion of grey.

Black and white are the only colours which really preserve the characteristic effect of another individual colour placed beside them, as they are neutral in effect and will isolate a colour if used to surround it.

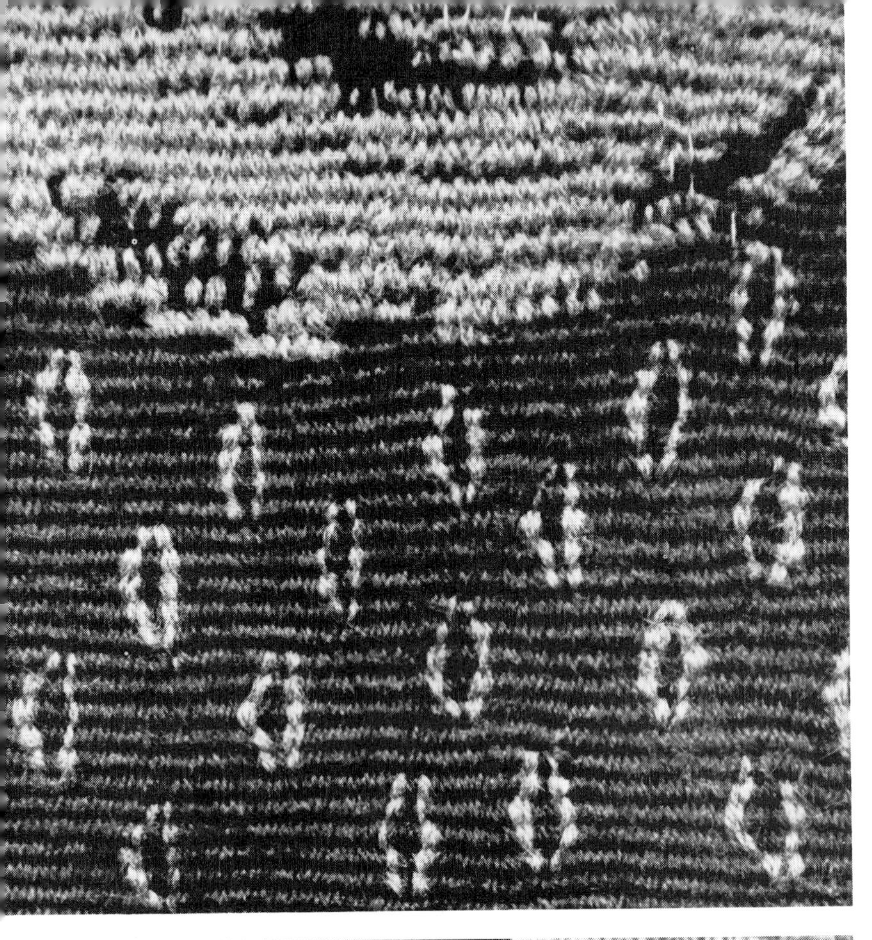

84 Stippling in two tones

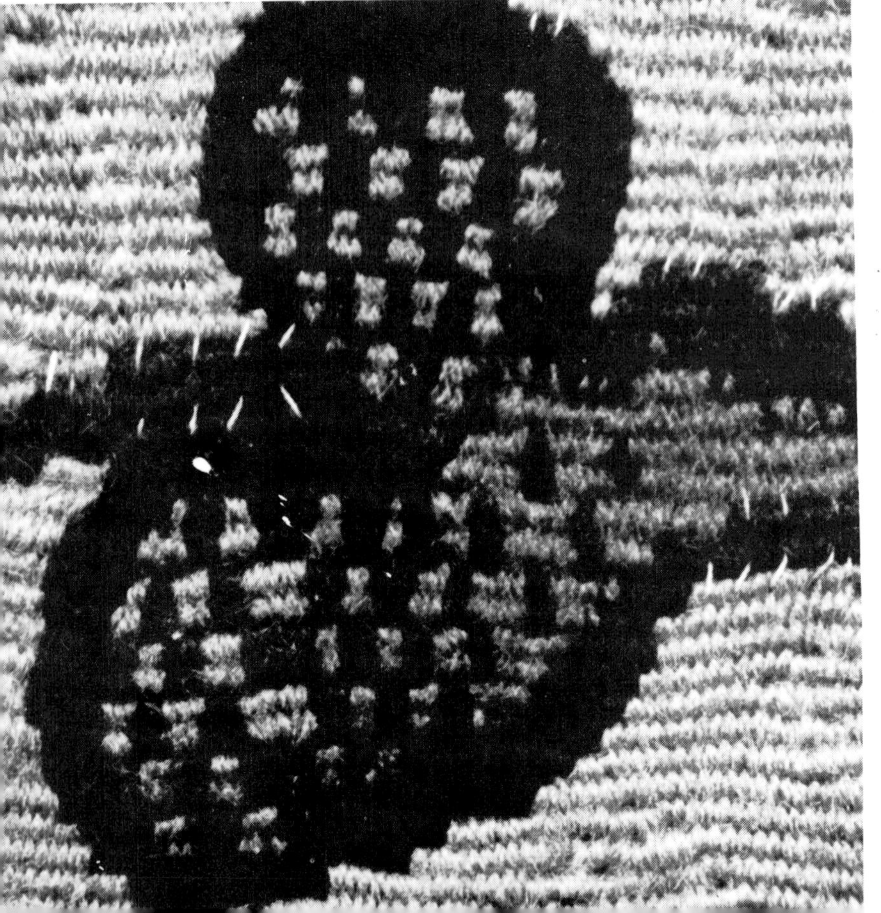

85 A leaf form with a chequered pattern produced by stippling

4 *The basic technique of tapestry weaving*

Tapestry weaving is basically one of the simplest methods of weaving and consists in picking up alternate warp threads and passing the weft thread beneath them in one direction, thus forming what is called a half-pass or shoot—also known in ordinary hand weaving as a pick—and then returning the weft thread to the point from which it started by taking it under the warp threads which before it passed over, and vice versa, so that it completes the full pass or course, as it has sometimes been called. There is, however, a difference between tapestry weaving and simple ordinary weaving in that the needle or bobbin carrying the weft is not taken straight across the full width of the warp at right angles and drawn tight, but is usually passed under only a few warp threads at a time, leaving an arc of the weft yarn, which is then knocked down by the weaver with the eye of the needle or the point of the bobbin until it completely covers the warp. This process of leaving a sufficient arc of weft to be knocked down so that it completely covers the warp leads to the formation of the ribs which are a distinguishing feature of the craft (see figure 86).

In this way a rep-type of material is produced; but this does not mean that rep is the same as tapestry. In the first place, rep can be produced mechanically, whereas real tapestry can only be produced by hand, and a second important difference between tapestry and plain rep, as also between it and other forms of hand weaving is that, except on rare occasions, no weft threads are taken to the full width of the design. Each area of pattern or of background is woven with a weft thread of the required colour, which is inserted between the warp threads and worked back and forth only over that section of the work where the particular colour appears on the design. This weft thread is then left hanging whilst another area of colour is worked but, when the original colour is again to be used, the first weft thread can be picked up once more and woven into the new area. A loop of the weft thread can be left between the two areas of weaving, provided it is not too long; otherwise, the thread should be cut off at the end of the first area of weaving with a short length

86 (LEFT) This figure shows how the warp threads are spaced by the weft, when the selvedge is formed. Also how an arc of weft thread is left to be knocked down to cover the warp completely, when the tapestry is being woven

87 (BELOW) A tapestry in the making. The weft is being built up to follow the curves of the design, which can be seen clearly, fixed beneath the warp threads. Ends of the weft threads are left hanging so that the side from which the weaver is working will become the back of the finished piece of work

88 Front view of the work in figure 87. The tracing of the design is turned back to show the finished surface. It also reveals how the design has dictated the order in which areas of colour should be built up

left hanging, and in the same way a short length of the thread should be left hanging at the point where the new area of weaving is commenced.

It follows that short ends or loops of the weft yarn will be left on the side of the tapestry from which the weaver is working, so that this side becomes the back of the finished panel. There is generally no need to darn in the ends of the weft thus left on the back of the work, as subsequent weft threads will hold them in position. Where a loose end of the weft would, however, be left hanging at the edge of the work, it is essential to weave it in for a short way from the edge.

The method of working one section of a design—one area of colour—at a time, and gradually building up shapes as one goes, brings certain limiting factors into the technique of tapestry weaving. The design tends, as it were, to dictate to the weaver which areas should be woven first, because, when one has to knock down the arc of the weft yarn each time one puts in a half-pass, it is important to be sure that all the warp threads below the area about to be worked have already been woven over, so that they can support the new weft. This entails building

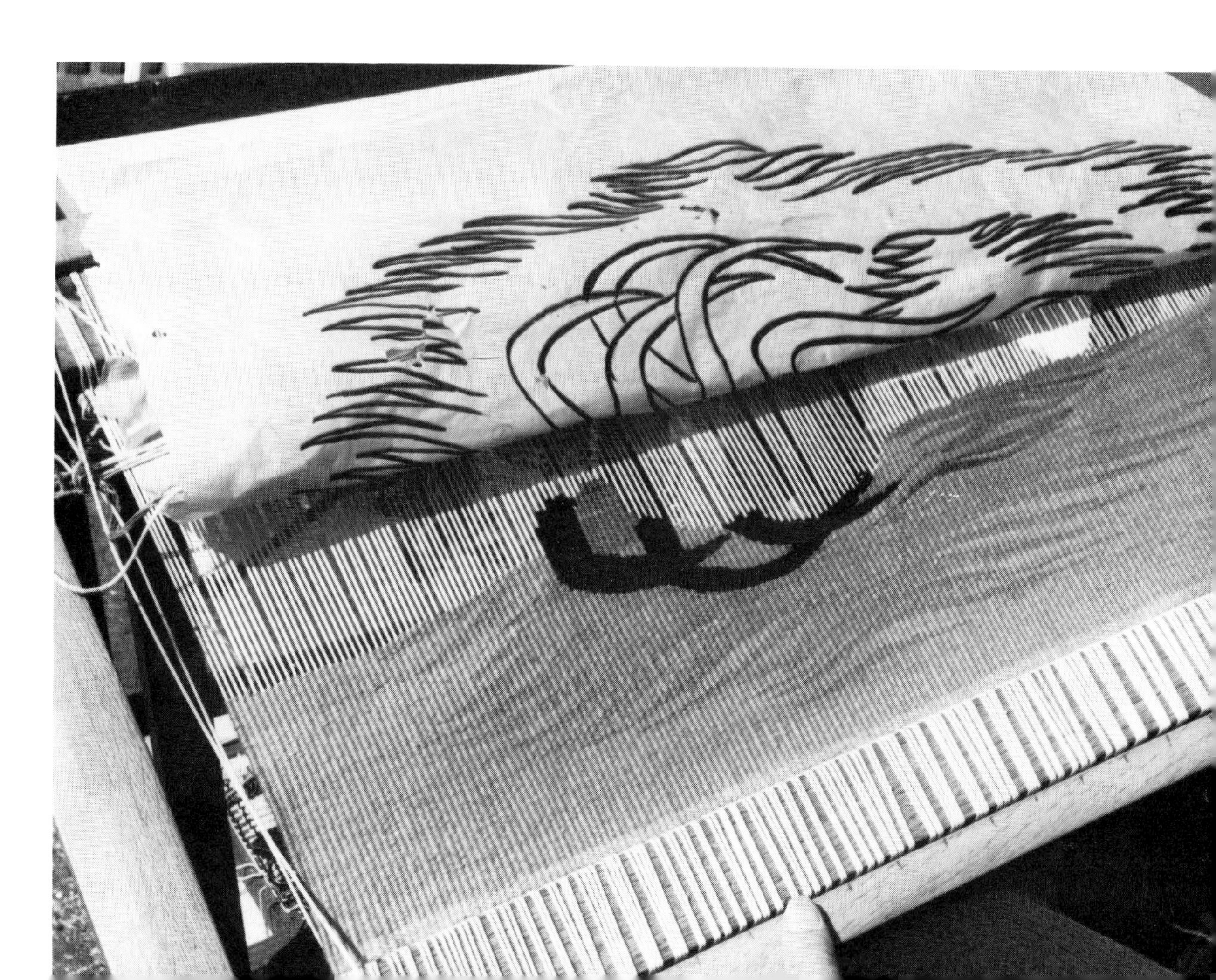

89 Detail showing how, in building up shapes in tapestry weaving, the weft threads may follow lines of colour in such a way that they may be woven diagonally to the warp direction. The result is to create strong, straight, diagonal lines (representing rays of sunlight) which could not have been achieved so effectively by weaving at right angles to the warp direction. However, great skill is needed to fit such a section of weaving satisfactorily into the rest of the work, without allowing it to weaken the fabric

up certain sections of the design before other over-lapping sections can be woven. Another feature which occurs as a result of this method of working is that a slit or turn-back is formed when the boundary of an area of colour is straight and lies parallel to the warp direction.

90 Detail showing bold, strong treatment of leaf shapes. It is a good example of the way shapes are built up, with the weft threads boldly following the curves of the leaves when strong contrasting shades are being used. When there is little colour contrast, stepped-slits outline the leaf forms

91 Lines of silk are woven in this detail (as in figure 90) diagonally across the warp threads, rather in the manner of the Coptic *crapaud*

Dealing with slits

When slits do occur, there are various methods of dealing with them. If they are felt to be helpful to a particular design, they can be left unstitched although, as we have already noticed, they can cause weakness in the fabric of a tapestry and may, therefore, in certain circumstances have to be sewn up. Where slits do not help the design, they can be sewn up when the work is ready to be removed from the frame or loom, in what was the traditional Western European way. This is done with fine thread from the back of the tapestry and is most easily accomplished whilst the work is still under slight tension (see figure 93). Sometimes, where slits are likely to be fairly long ones and may cause difficulty during actual weaving, it is a good idea to sew them up as the work proceeds.

92 (LEFT) Here slits can be seen which do not help the design in any way. They will, therefore, need to be sewn up

93 (RIGHT) Traditional method of sewing up slits

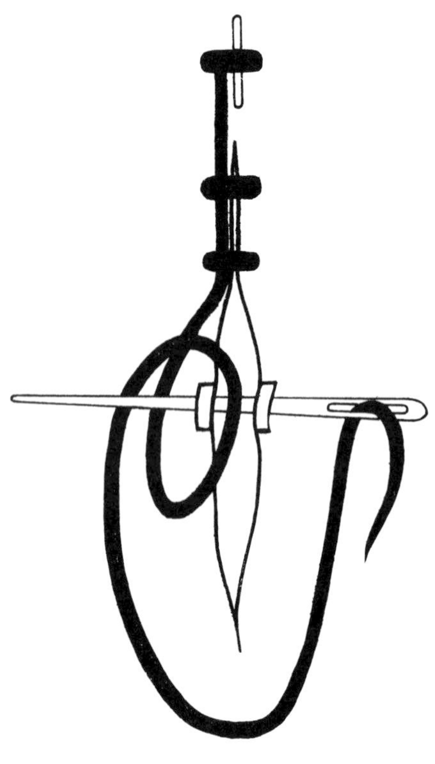

94a (LEFT) *Comb-dovetailing*, with one thread of each colour alternating over a common warp thread

94b (RIGHT) An example of *comb-dovetailing*

There are several ways of avoiding the occurrence of slits during weaving. One way is to dovetail adjoining areas of colour into one another by passing the weft in turn first from one side and then from the other over a common warp. This method is generally called *comb-dovetailing*, and it can also be done by taking several weft threads first from one side and then from the other over a common warp thread (see figure 94). This is not, however, a very satisfactory method, unless, of course, the effect created fits in well with the design being woven, as not only does the fabric build up at the point of juncture but the outline of the design also becomes somewhat blurred. Slits can also be avoided by causing the threads of weft in adjoining areas of colour not to turn back in each pass at the same point, but to alternate between two adjacent warp threads (see figure 96). This method, which is another form of dovetailing, sometimes called *teething*, avoids build up of weft along the join, but still gives a slightly blurred outline.

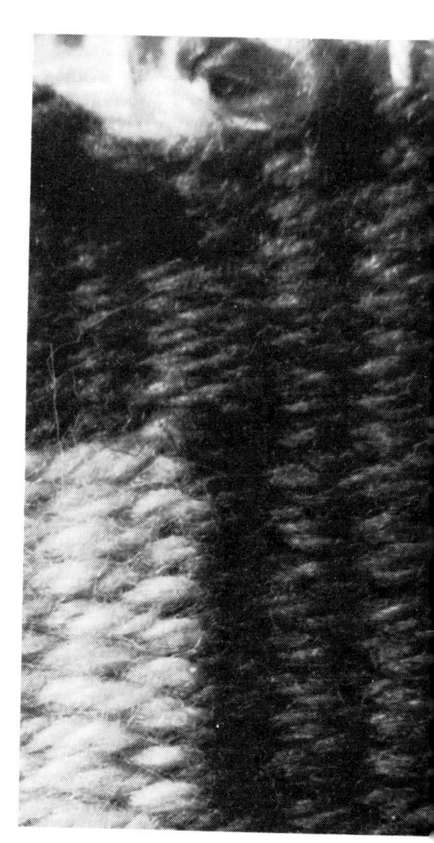

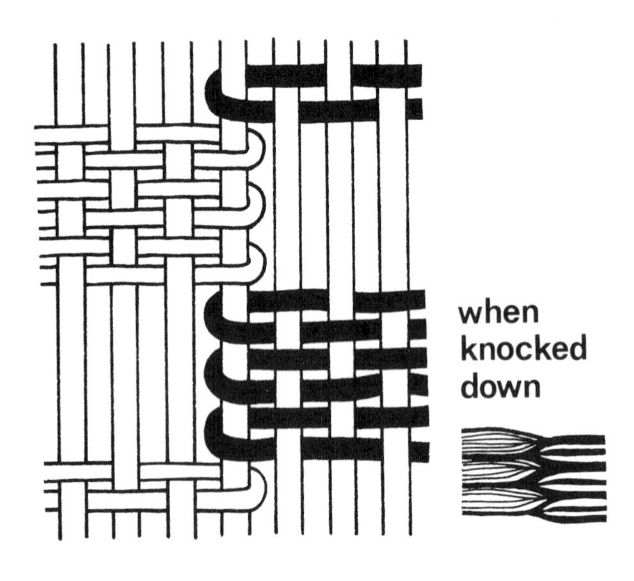

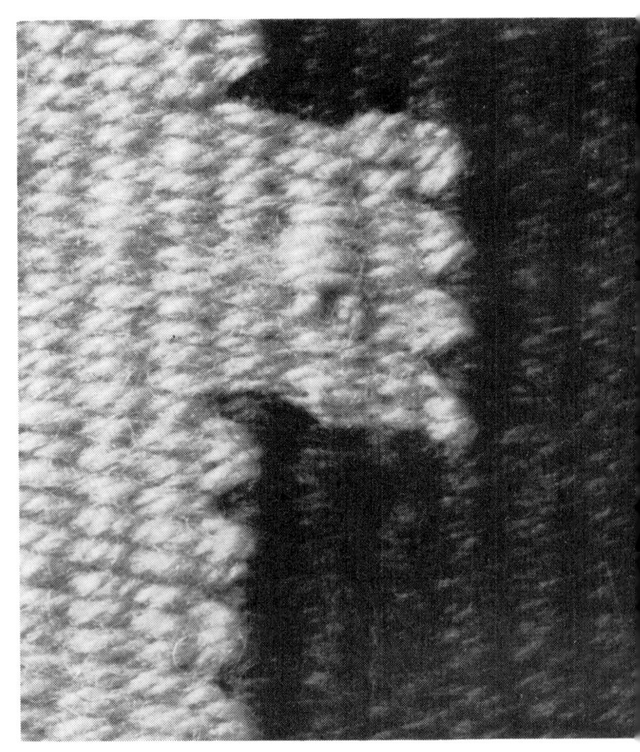

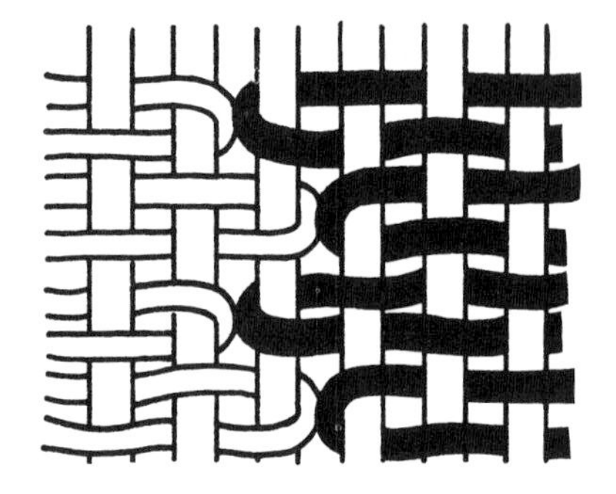

95a (ABOVE LEFT) *Comb-dovetailing in clusters*. Sometimes called saw-tooth dovetailing

95b (ABOVE RIGHT) An example of *comb-dovetailing in clusters*

96 (LEFT) *Teething*

Interlocking the weft

Another slightly more complicated method of avoiding slits whilst weaving is in progress involves interlocking the weft threads. Starting with a thread of the colour which is on the left-hand side of the point where two areas of colour are to meet along the line of the warp, it is necessary to weave with this colour towards the right until the point of juncture is reached. Here the thread of the first colour is left hanging and the second colour is taken and with it the weaving is continued in the same shed to the right-hand edge of the second area of colour, the initial end of this thread having been left hanging over and to the left of the hanging thread of the first colour. Then the thread of the second colour is woven back from the right until it returns to the point of juncture, where it is left hanging on the left-hand side of the first colour. The hanging thread of this first colour is then carried over the two hanging threads of the other colour, and the weaving is continued with it to the left-hand edge of its own area of colour and back again to the point of juncture, where it is left hanging to the right of the other coloured threads. The process is completed by taking up the nearer end of the second colour and weaving with it to the right and back again to the centre and then continuing in the same sequence until the particular area of the design is woven in. It will then be observed that the two areas of colour are firmly interlocked and meet along a clear dividing line (see figures 98 and 99). This method of avoiding slits by interlocking (which, although it sounds very complicated, is in reality quite easy to master) was introduced at the Gobelin Manufactory in the eighteenth century and was very highly thought of at the time, because the finished tapestry was then considered to resemble a painting more closely!

97 Weft threads linked between two warp threads

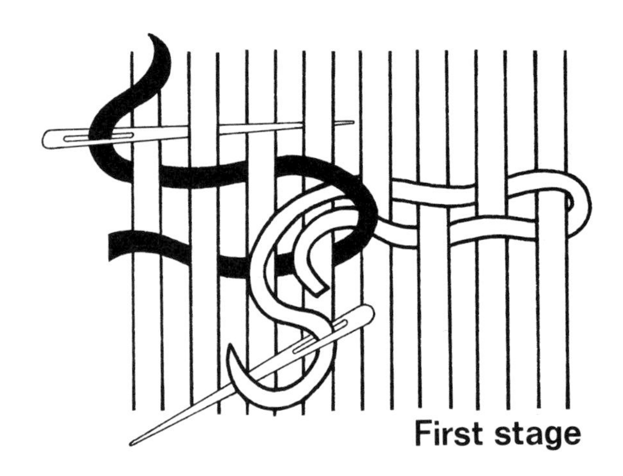

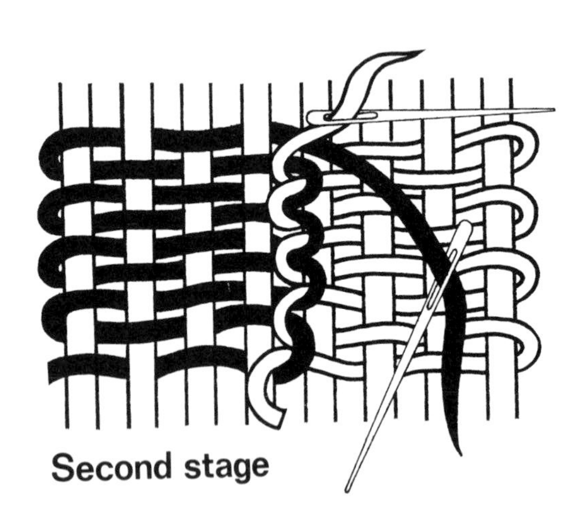

98a and b Interlocking of the weft

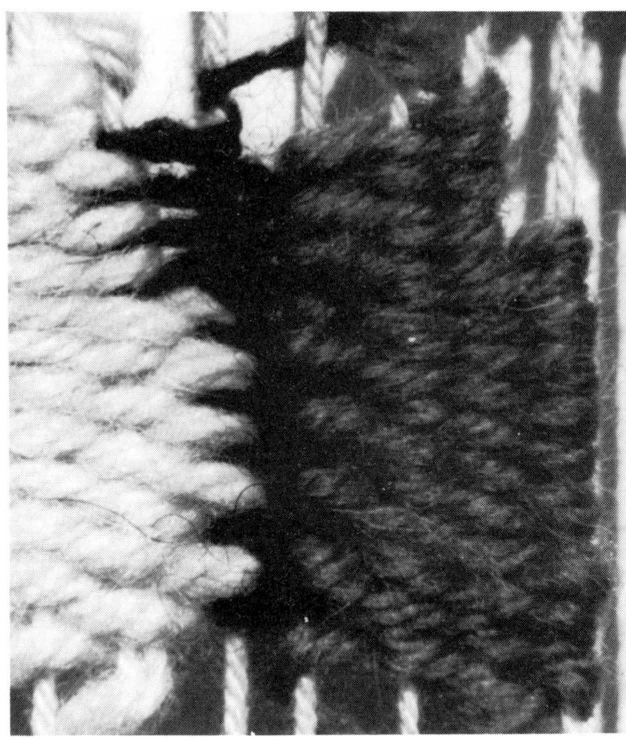

99 (LEFT) Interlocking viewed from the back of the work

100 (RIGHT) Stitching up by means of outline stitch, as in early Peruvian weaving

Further ways of dealing with slits

There is a further method, found in early Peruvian weaving, whereby a black outline weft was dovetailed over two warp threads, one in each of the adjacent areas of colour, and this not only avoided the formation of slits, but also kept the outline of the design clear (see figure 100). The same method was used in sixteenth century Persian silk tapestry rugs.

Finally, I can see no good reason why a transparent sewing thread should not today be used to weave a full pass right across two such adjacent areas of colour after every two passes of weft, in order to close an unwanted slit. This thread would be strong and thin enough not to build up, and would disappear under the weft when knocked down.

The problem of two weft threads in the same shed

Another problem which occurs in weaving tapestry, when individual areas of colour are built up before other adjacent ones have been started, is that it will often be found, when a new weft thread is about to be put in above one of a different colour, that the two weft threads will pass through the same shed—that is, they will be lying directly one above the other and passing over and under the same warp threads. This is not good because, when the weft is knocked down, some parts of alternate warps will not be completely covered on the front of the work. It is necessary, therefore, to stop on such an occasion and look for a way of overcoming the difficulty. It may perhaps be possible to add or to take out one half-pass of the first colour in order to put the new weft thread into the correct shed but, if for some reason this appears undesirable, and the area where the two weft threads would be in the same shed is only a small one, it is quite practicable to let the new weft thread pass over the back of these particular warp threads, and then, when it returns in the reverse shed, everything will be correct again, and it will be possible to continue weaving straight on without trouble (see figure 101).

A method which I employ, when this problem arises, is to proceed as follows: if the first warp thread, at which the new weft thread would pass into the wrong shed, is already covered by the previous weft thread on the front side of the work, I allow the new weft thread to jump over it instead of passing under it, and then weave straight on; but, if this particular warp

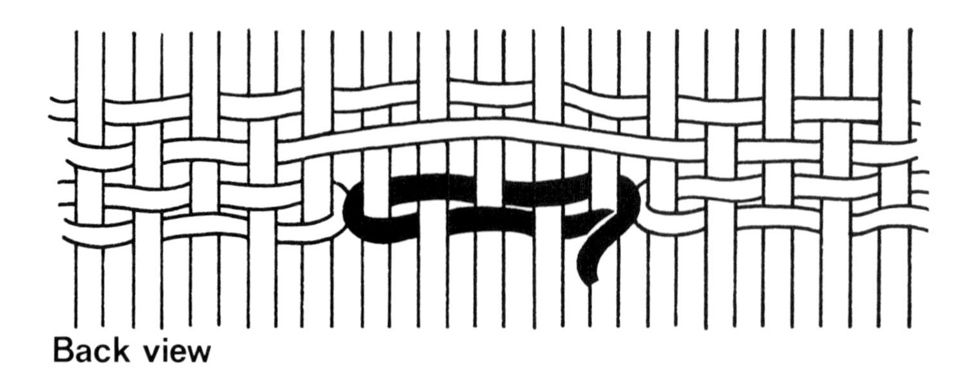

101 A method of correcting the problem of two weft threads passing through the same shed

thread has not been covered by the previous weft on the front side of the work, I make the new weft thread, which would normally have passed over it, wrap round it and then jump over the following warp thread (see figure 102). By this method an even number of weft threads is kept on the front of each warp thread, but the process of avoiding putting the weft into the wrong shed must be repeated each time the weft thread passes over the difficult area.

Floating weft threads

When making corrections to avoid passing two weft threads through the same shed, it is necessary to watch carefully that no unwanted floating threads appear upon the front surface of the work. These floating threads, which occur as the result of passing the weft under more than one warp thread at a time, are sometimes introduced purposely in order to produce an unusual textural effect, but they will also occur when they are not desired, if the weaver fails to pay careful enough attention to the process of weaving. They can, however, be easily corrected once discovered, by adopting the following procedure: weave in another weft thread of the same colour in the same shed beside the floating weft, beginning 25 mm (1 in.) on one side of it and finishing the same distance on the other side. Then cut the floating thread and pull the ends through to the back of the work.

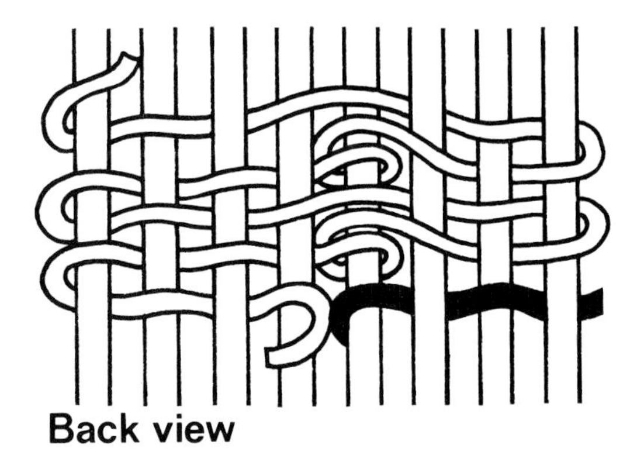

102 An alternative method of avoiding two weft threads in the same shed

Dark hatchings shading into light

Hachure

Hachure, which is a method of shading from one colour into another by the formation of thin spire-shaped areas of colour known as hatchings, presents little difficulty to the weaver. To form an individual hatching a full pass of weft in the chosen colour is woven from right to left up to the full length of the hatching required and back; then a second pass is put in with the same coloured weft above this first one, but this time the turn-back is a few warp threads short of the first one. Other passes of the same kind are added, each one turning back a few warp threads short of the turn-back before it, until the complete elongated triangle shape of the hatching has been woven. Now the weft thread of the second colour is woven in from left to right until it meets the turn-back of the first pass of the other colour, where it also turns back and returns to make a second pass, which this time will be a few warp threads longer than the first pass and will, therefore, be woven over part of the first pass of the other colour and will not turn back until it meets the turn-back of the second pass of the first colour. In this way successive passes of the second colour will form a hatching which is the reverse of the one already worked in the first colour and which will fit exactly over it, finally completing a row of weft right across the whole width of the warp threads in use. This process is repeated as often as is necessary to produce the area of hachure required (see figure 103).

103 The method of working hatchings

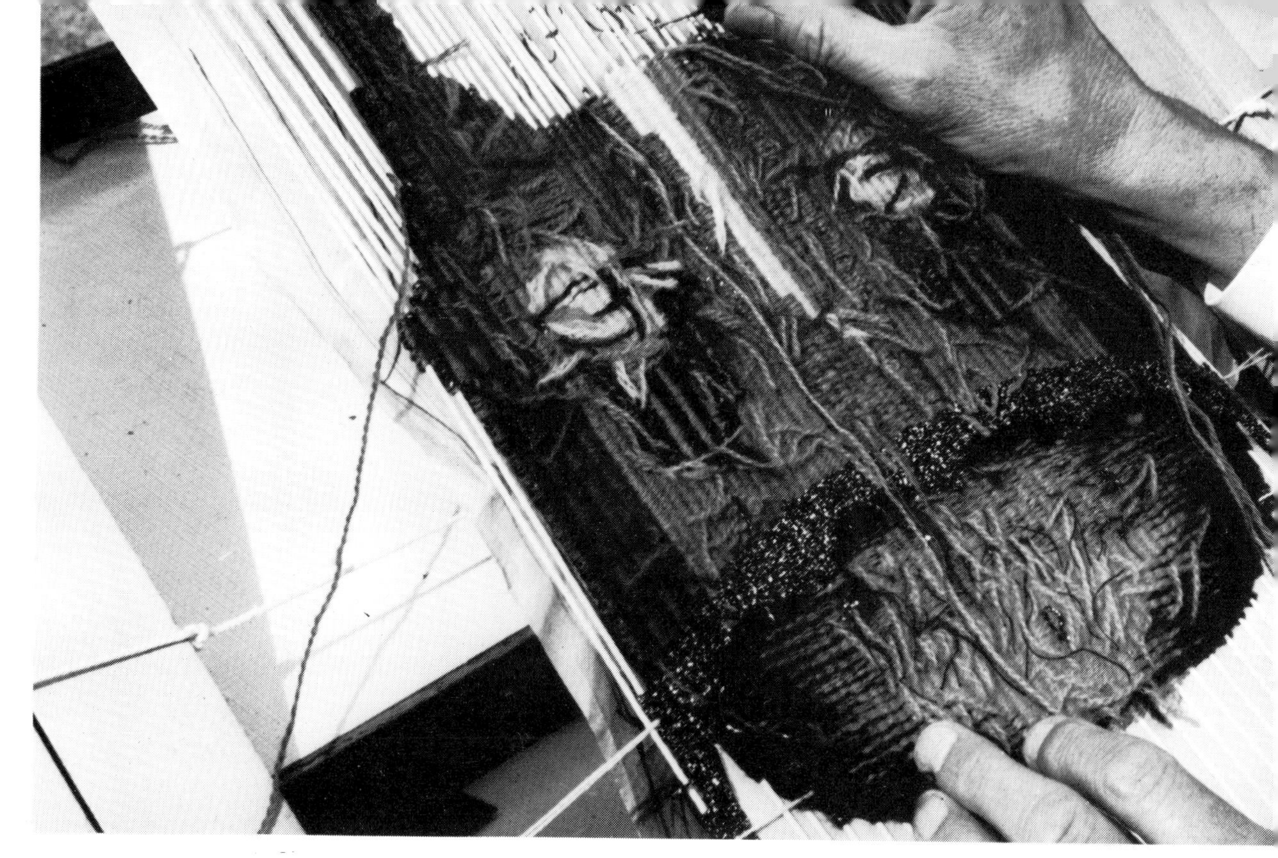

Weaving circular or irregular shapes in tapestry upon a rectangular frame

It is often quite intriguing to get right away from weaving rectangular panels and to try weaving pieces which are circular in outline, or which have some more irregular shape. To do this on a rectangular frame, however, it is necessary to remember what we have already discovered, when building up shapes in tapestry on such a frame or loom, that areas of weft cannot be knocked down on to other areas where the warp remains bare. This problem can nevertheless be overcome by taking a rectangular piece of thin card and cutting out of its top edge the lower half of the shape, such as a circle, which is to be woven. This card with the shape cut out of it should then be put through the warp threads so that it lies in one shed in the position required and it will form a basis upon which the weft threads may be knocked down (see figure 104).

104 Here an irregularly-shaped tapestry is being woven. At the base of the weaving, a thin cardboard shape can be seen placed between the warp threads. The weft thread has been knocked down on this shape. Such a cardboard shape is not required at the top of the frame, since there is now a firm basis of woven fabric onto which new weft threads may be knocked down

The upper section of a circular shape, as of many irregular shapes, can easily be woven, as it can be built up on the weft below, but if holes are to be left somewhere in the middle of a design, it will again be necessary to cut out their shapes in thin card and to place these at the points in the work where the holes are to occur, fitting them through the warp threads in a similar manner to that mentioned above.

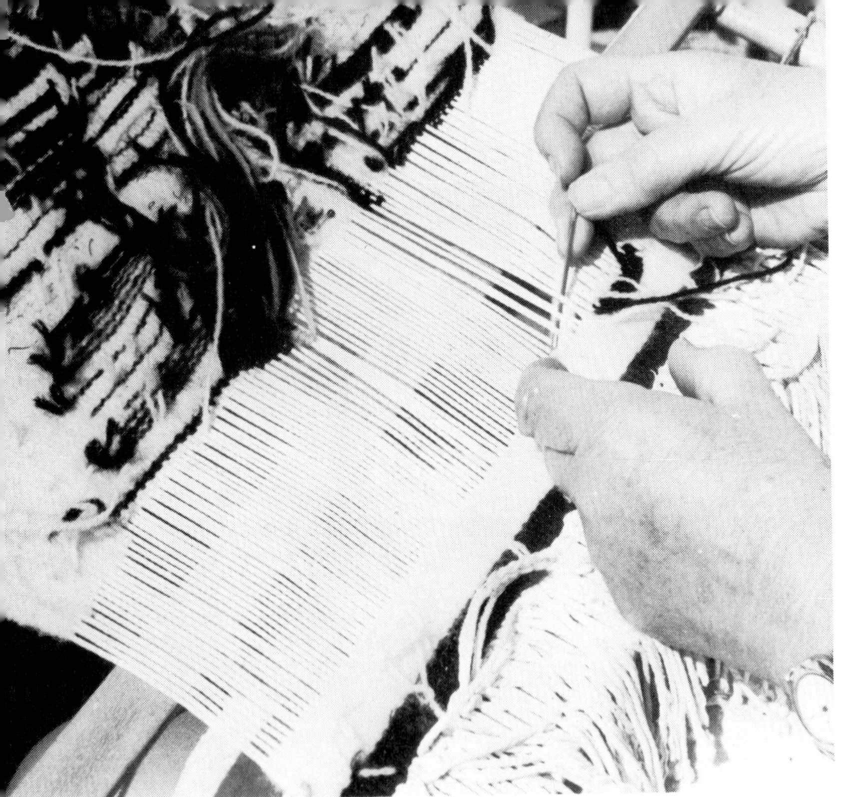

105 The weaver has reversed the frame and is working from the other end because she has experienced difficulty in weaving the final section from the original end

106 The completed panel shown in figure 105. *Zena Halliwell*

107 This shows how waisting of the tapestry can be avoided during weaving by tying the edges of the woven material to the sides of the frame at intervals, as the work progresses

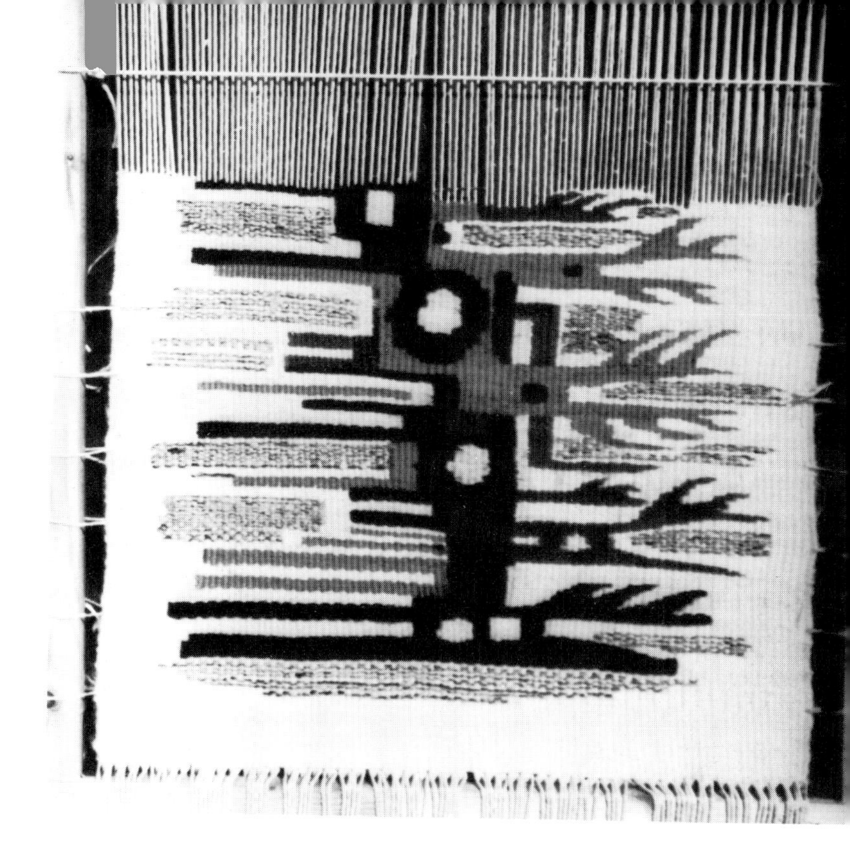

108 This shows how the width of a woven panel can also increase towards the centre of the work during weaving

Keeping an even width in the woven tapestry

When weaving a panel of tapestry, it is necessary to watch the width of the piece carefully, as the work progresses. There is a tendency, especially when long warp threads are being used, for the tapestry to develop a 'waist'. This is due to the fact that, while the warp threads are held in position by being tied to the bars of the frame at the top and bottom of the work, they have nothing to support them in the middle section. If an insufficient arc of weft is left by the weaver, and particularly if silk or a tightly spun yarn is used, then the tension may cause the warp threads to draw more closely together as the work progresses.

To avoid this waisting, ties should be introduced every so often during weaving. These are short lengths of twine, which should be attached to the sides of the work by being passed through the selvedge warps and should then be tied to the sides of the frame and drawn tight in order to keep the width of the work constant.

Strangely enough an effect which is the opposite of waisting sometimes occurs when one is working on small frames and, instead of the warp threads being pulled in, the width of the woven panel increases towards the centre. This happens generally where the piece of work has an area of plain background weaving at the beginning and at the end, and where the design in the centre calls for numerous colour changes, entailing many turn-backs.

The only way to avoid the occurrence of this effect is to keep a constant watch and to vary the tension where necessary by leaving a slightly smaller arc of weft yarn to be knocked down, if the width of the work appears to be increasing or, if possible, to use a harder and more tightly spun wool, or silk in place of wool, when weaving the central portions of a panel, where this problem is likely to arise.

109 A panel worked in black and white wool and cotton, together with silver lurex. Many warps in the centre have been wrapped and this section shows the clever treatment of a design which has both vertical and horizontal lines. *Lilian Hill*

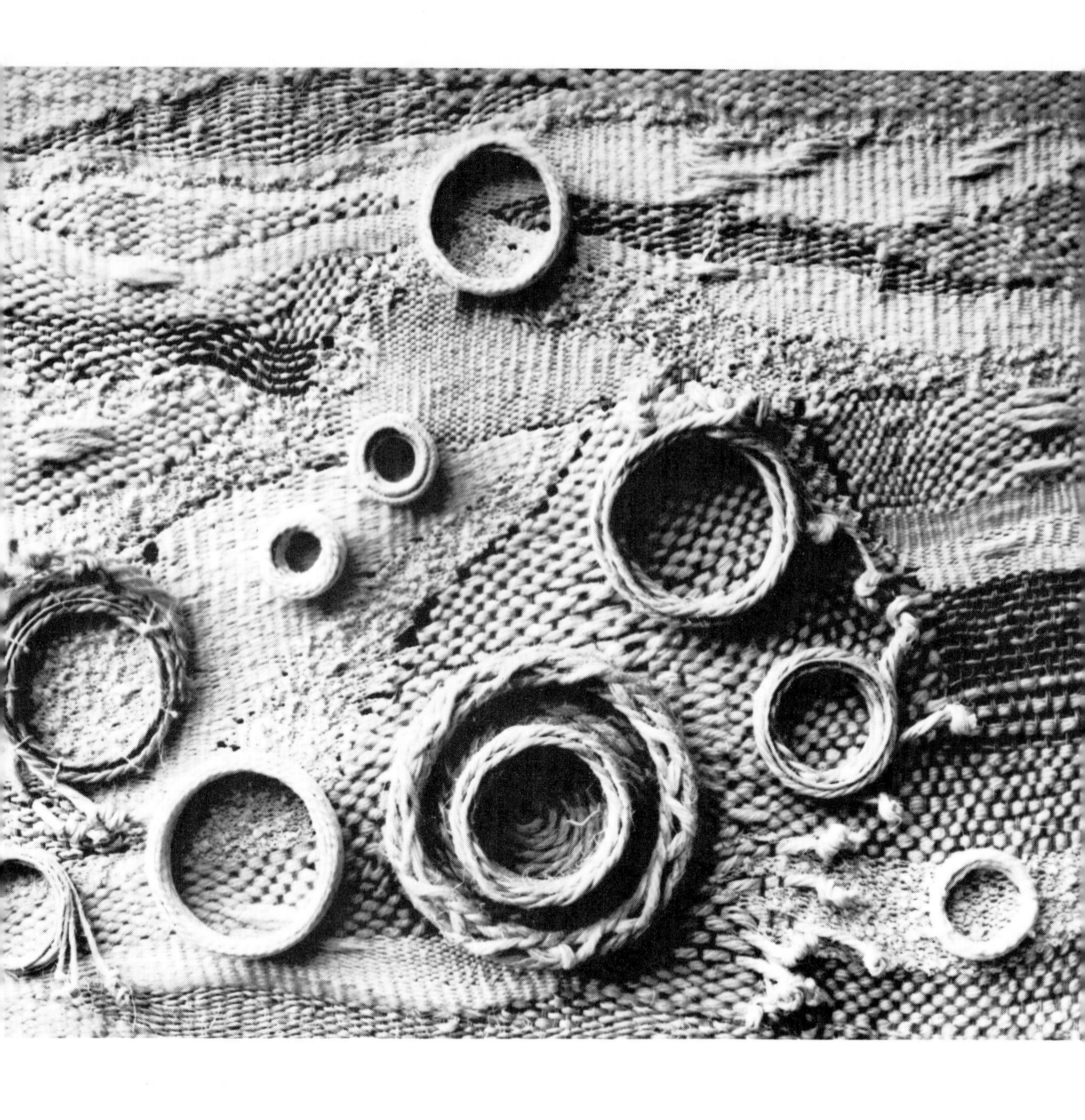

110 *Sea of Tranquillity* by *Winnie Browning*. Freely-woven panel using various twines, including sisal, bouclé wool and cotton

5 *Materials and their employment in working on small frames*

Many different types of material are available today for weaving tapestries, and it is necessary to be fully aware of their special individual qualities before deciding which to use for a given purpose, as the nature of the materials used can influence the quality of the finished woven fabric very considerably and can impart a particular characteristic to its texture and general appearance.

Warp

Any yarn can be used for warp provided it is strong, smooth, tightly twisted and—a most important point—provided it possesses a certain elasticity. The thickness of the warp should depend solely upon the nature of the design, and I believe that the coarsest possible warp should be chosen upon which the weaver is able comfortably to interpret all the details of a particular design. There is no special virtue in choosing a fine warp just for fineness' sake. A warp, in fact, which is finer than it need be can cause a design to lose character and to appear flat and insipid. This is because the ribbed effect produced by the warp threads will then be much less pronounced, and there will be a general lack of vigour.

Wool warp

In the past it was quite common to use strong, fine, tightly-spun wool for the warp as well as for the weft, and today wool can still make an excellent warp material, if it is handled with great care. It is naturally much softer than a cotton warp and, if care is not taken, the work may be pulled out of shape, but it also has a real asset in its pronounced elasticity, which helps greatly with the placing of the weft threads, so that very lively and interesting effects can result from its use. This special quality of elasticity will, however, be easily lost, if wool warp is over-stretched.

Cotton warp

Cotton twine is the main yarn used today for the warp in tapestry weaving, as it meets all the requirements for a warp material. Cotton threads provide a particularly firm kind of warp material and they are, therefore, very easy to keep evenly placed on the frame or loom in use. A really coarse rounded cotton warp can also give a very lively surface to the finished work as a result of the distinct ribs which it creates.

Linen warp

Linen warps were used in certain ancient tapestries and are still sometimes used today. Most weavers, however, now avoid using linen as, owing to its lack of elasticity, it is somewhat difficult to use and is liable to break during weaving.

Silk warp

Spun or plied silk is strong and was used in the past by the Chinese for their all-silk tapestries, but I think we would all agree that to use pure silk today for a warp which is to be entirely covered by the weft would indeed be an extravagance. We should probably think it much wiser to use silk only as a weft material.

Rayon warp

Rayon is strong as a warp material, but it is non-elastic.

Nylon warp

Nylon is also a strong warp material, but it is exceedingly difficult to keep the tension of nylon warp threads even: they have a distinct tendency to slip, and the knots cannot be kept tied tightly enough.

Weft

A great variety of materials may be employed today as weft for tapestry weaving. As in the case of warp materials, however, they should be chosen to suit the purpose for which the tapestry is to be used, and also to suit the design to be interpreted. In working the more conventional type of tapestry the weft material should, of course, be of a kind that can easily be knocked down to cover the warp and should be of a durable enough quality to withstand the wear which the finished piece of work might be expected to encounter.

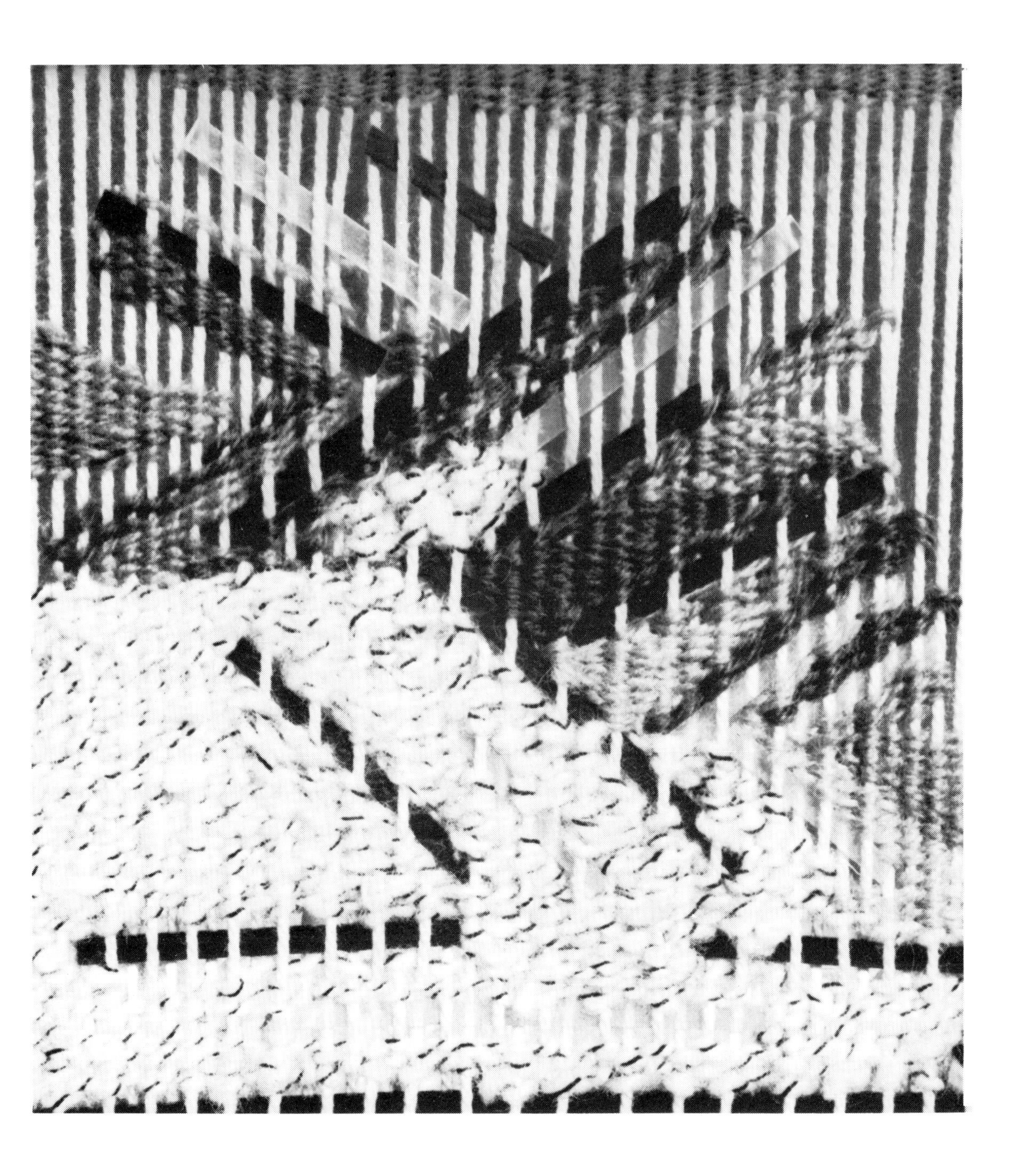

111 Part of an unfinished panel, showing narrow strips of perspex woven in with a novelty wool

Wool weft

The basic material employed as weft in the production of tapestry in the past was wool, and it remains so to the present day. Wool is unsurpassed by any other fibre for its wonderful tactile qualities. These, combined with its great elasticity, liveliness and its sheer beauty when woven, give tapestry its true character. All tightly spun wools are ideal for tapestry weaving, as they impart a firm, clean, well-defined appearance to the weaving. A loosely spun wool, being slightly hairy, gives a more fuzzy look, but it is very easy to work with and it knocks down well, completely covering the warp threads. Carpet thrums, which are rather more hairy, are possible on coarse warp and, if the final effect of hairiness they give is unacceptable, a lighted taper, carefully passed over the surface when the tapestry is completed, will soon remedy the state of affairs. Various types of knitting wool—two, three and four ply—can also be useful, as can the small skeins of tapestry (four ply) and crewel (two ply) wool. The only type of wool which is unsuitable for tapestry weaving is the very soft type of so-called baby wool.

Silk weft

Silk is used mainly to highlight certain areas in a tapestry, as it contrasts exceedingly well with wool. It is often mixed in the needle with wool and, when so used, gives to the weaving a bright and luxuriant appearance. Tapestries like the Chinese ones, however, in which silk is used exclusively as the weft material, have not the same lively appearance as those in which silk and wool are combined: they appear flat and are lacking in tactile qualities.

Metal threads as weft

Gold and silver threads can be used in small quantities, but care should be exercised when using real silver thread, as this is liable to tarnish and will eventually go black. Unless, therefore, the design would look equally well worked in black, it would be advisable to reconsider using real silver thread, and it might be advantageous to look around for a synthetic type of metal yarn. *Twilley's Goldfingering* can also be useful here. This is a mixture of metallised polyester with other synthetic threads and is available at the present time not only in gold, but also in silver and bronze, mixed with threads in a variety of different colours such as blue, green, pink and occasionally black. This type of yarn is a fashion product, principally in use for knitting purposes, and as such it will remain on the market only as long as the fashion for it lasts, so it is always wise to buy these fibres where and when they are available, and thus to build up a stock of interesting threads, for once they have gone off the market, they will have gone for good—at least, in their present form.

Cotton weft

Various cotton yarns are also useful in small quantities as weft material, although cotton does appear somewhat heavy and dull compared with wool and silk.

Other weft materials

While a plain, tightly twisted wool is the most suitable yarn for weaving tapestry, for the freer type of work now being produced which, although it may be described as tapestry, often bears little or no resemblance to the true tapestry we know from the past, almost any long, straight fibre can be used. Simply anything which is capable of being put through the warp threads is used as weft: string of all thicknesses and colours, horsehair, mohair, rya, camel hair, poodles' hair, perlé, bouclé, natural fibres such as raffia, jute, sisal and hemp, wood shavings, strips of tree bark, twigs, stalks of dried plants and grasses, paper, plastic materials of all kinds, beads threaded on the weft thread and a vast range of synthetic yarns. The choice is almost limitless and gives to the present-day tapestry weaver an ever-increasing and quite bewildering selection.

It is wise, however, to rein in the desire to acquire everything which attracts the attention and to buy just those materials which appear to be unusual either in colour or in texture. Many suitable wools and yarns are to be found in large stores and wool shops, but some are more difficult to locate and can only be purchased from time to time. It is always worthwhile, when on holiday in other countries, to visit the local markets to look for unusual yarns to use as weft materials.

112 Detail of a black, white and blue hanging. Wooden beads are threaded on to certain warp threads and narrow strips of coloured perspex are inserted at intervals through the warp

Frames and looms

Weaving a tapestry on a small scale requires no elaborate or expensive equipment: it can be accomplished by making a simple, strong, rigid, rectangular frame upon which to fix the warp. This frame should have a width which is slightly more than the width of warp to be used and ideally should be about 23 cm (9 in.) longer than the maximum length of warp required in the finished piece of work (see figure 113). Picture frames, provided they are strong enough for the purpose, can also be used, as can rug-making frames and any loom, in fact, on which it is possible to do ordinary tabby weave.

Some students of mine have had made for them very sturdy wooden frames which measure approximately 91 cm × 50 cm (36 in. × 20 in.) and which they can easily transport from place to place. These frames have two side struts, measuring approximately 50 cm × 44 mm × 22 mm (20 in. × $1\frac{3}{4}$ in. × $\frac{7}{8}$ in.), and each of these has two holes at either end, one about 50 mm (2 in.) in from the end and the other 95 mm ($3\frac{3}{4}$ in.) in, to take round-headed bolts and wing nuts. Two wooden cross bars are attached to these side struts at each end by means of the bolts and wing nuts, the outer bar being approximately 91 cm × 25 mm × 25 mm (36 in. × 1 in. × 1 in.), and the inner bar approximately 91 cm × 50 mm × 25 mm (36 in. × 2 in. × 1 in.). When the two inner bars have been attached to the side struts by means of the nuts and bolts, the whole frame is kept square by four small rectangular brackets fixed to the side struts and also attached to the two inner bars (see figure 114).

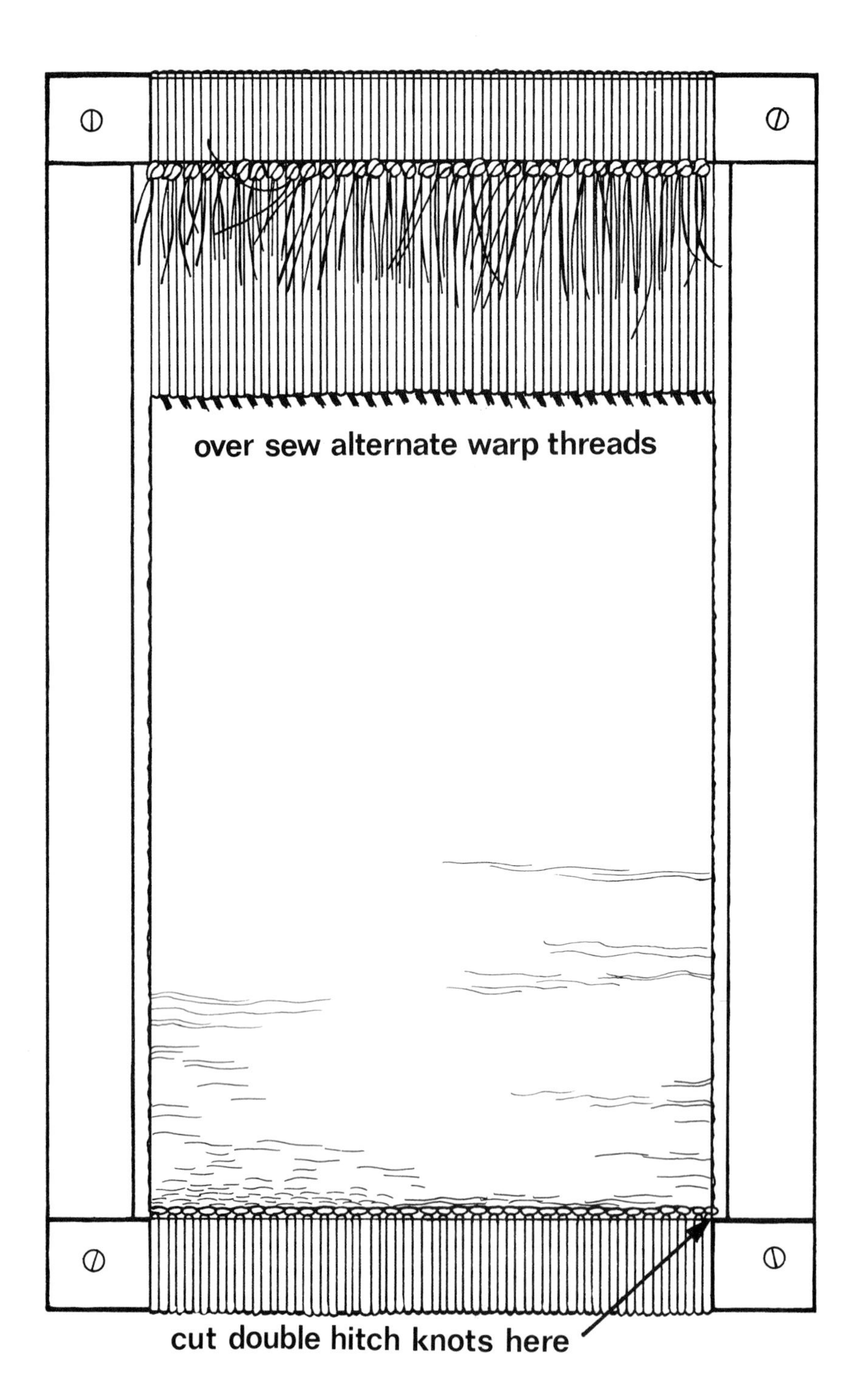
over sew alternate warp threads
cut double hitch knots here

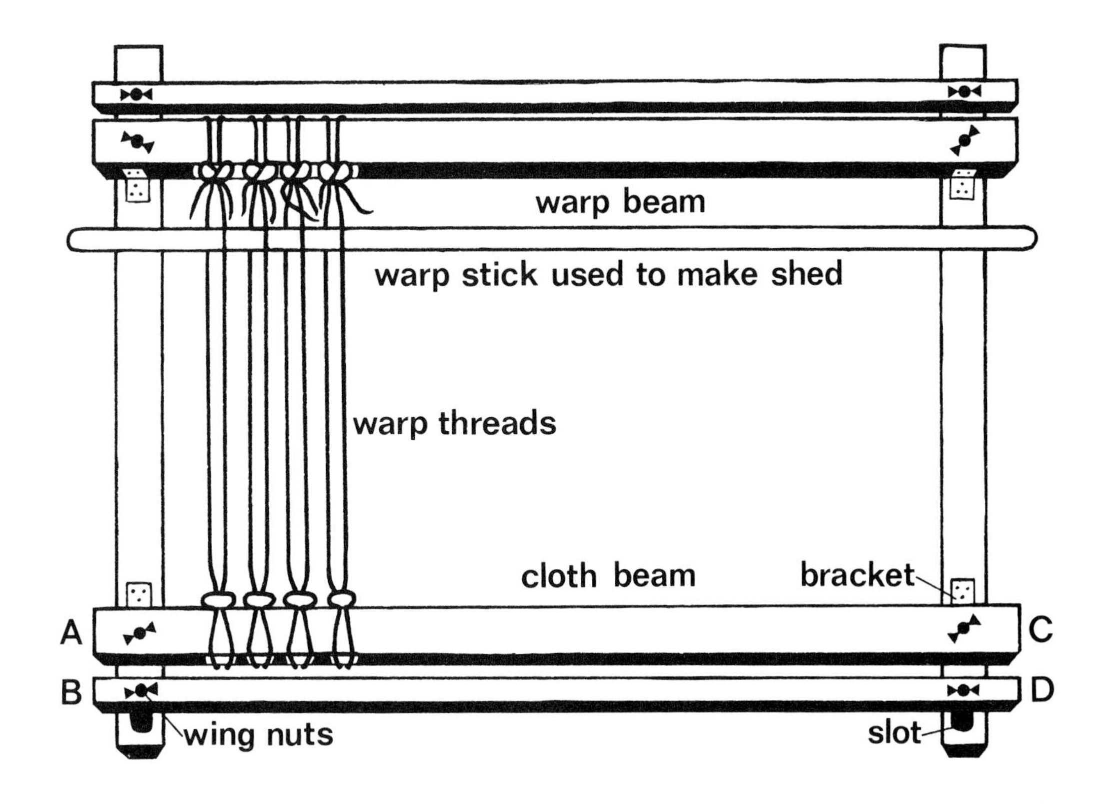

The inner wooden cross bars on this frame serve as cloth and warp beams, and can be released from the frame, when as much as possible of the weaving has been done and a further length is still to be woven. The cloth beam can be rotated in order to wind up the section of tapestry already worked and can then be re-attached to the frame. The warp is then adjusted and the warp beam is itself re-attached to the frame. By this means a weaver, with a frame which measures only 91 cm × 50 cm (36 in. × 20 in.), can work a piece of tapestry in which the maximum width of the warp will be about 76 cm (30 in.) and the length of the warp will simply depend upon how much warp—within reason—the weaver wishes to attach to the frame. Obviously, there must be sufficient space left between the cloth beam and the other cross bar on that side of the frame to enable the tapestry to be wound up on the cloth beam. A way of making sure that a reasonable space will be left would be to make a slot instead of a round hole for the bolts at points B and D on the side struts (see figure 114). This would allow the position of the outer cross bar adjacent to the cloth beam to be adjusted as required.

113 (OPPOSITE) A simple, rectangular frame, showing the size of the frame in comparison with the tapestry to be woven

114 (ABOVE) A strong portable frame with warp and cloth beams which allows larger pieces of tapestry to be woven than does the simple rectangular frame

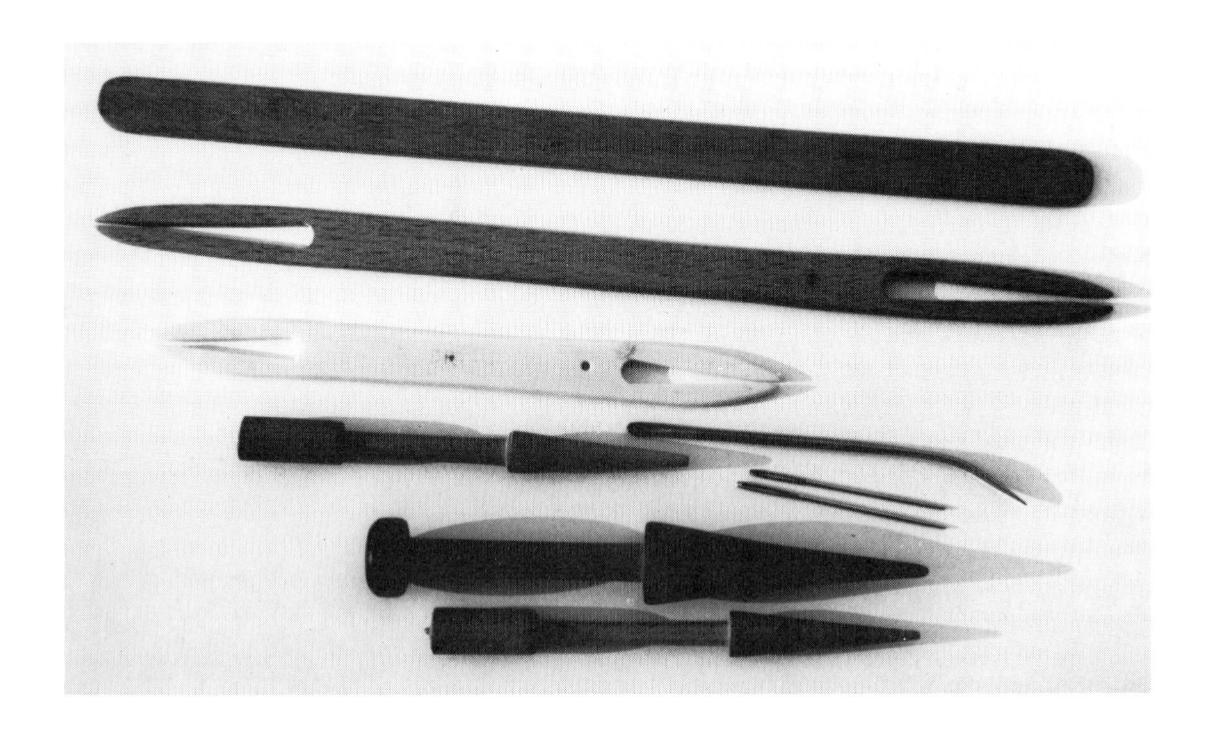

A flat stick, known as a warpstick or shedstick, is needed for use with this tapestry frame. It should be as long as the full width of the frame, so that it rests comfortably on the side struts, and should be about 25 mm (1 in.) in width. This, together with a ball of string big enough to supply the warp, a packet of large-eyed, blunt-pointed tapestry needles—suggested size 18—and a varied collection of interesting woollen and other yarns for the weft, is all that is required to commence weaving the chosen design. If, however, there are large areas of one colour to be woven, it would be helpful to have a shuttle or bobbin which holds a larger amount of weft thread than a needle (see figure 115).

Anyone preferring to have a tapestry frame which is somewhat more solid than the wooden frame described above and which is capable of standing on its own legs, whilst not being too big and heavy to transport, could have made for them a strong metal frame with retractable legs such as that illustrated in figure 116. This frame was designed by Mr Archie Brennan of the Edinburgh Tapestry Company as a free-standing yet portable loom for weaving smaller tapestries, and its overall dimensions are 91 cm × 76 cm (36 in. × 30 in.).

115 (ABOVE) A warpstick, shuttles, needles and bobbins of the types used in working small tapestries

116 (OPPOSITE) A strong metal frame with retractable legs, designed by *Archie Brennan* of the *Edinburgh Tapestry Company* for weaving small tapestries. The overall dimensions of the frame (when the legs are retracted) are 91 cm × 76 cm (36 in. × 30 in.)

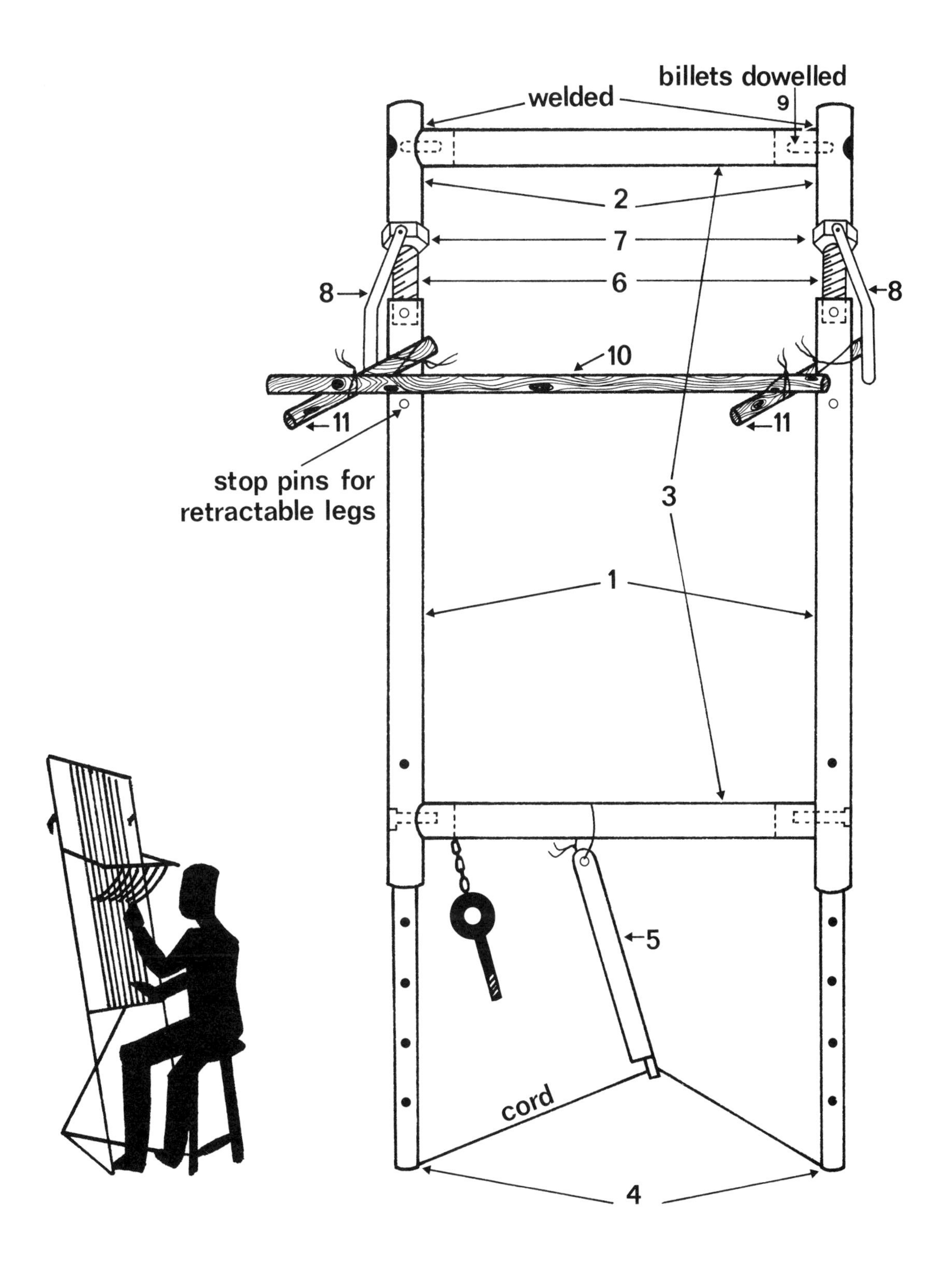
billets dowelled
welded
9
2
7
6
8
8
10
11
11
stop pins for
retractable legs
3
1
5
cord
4

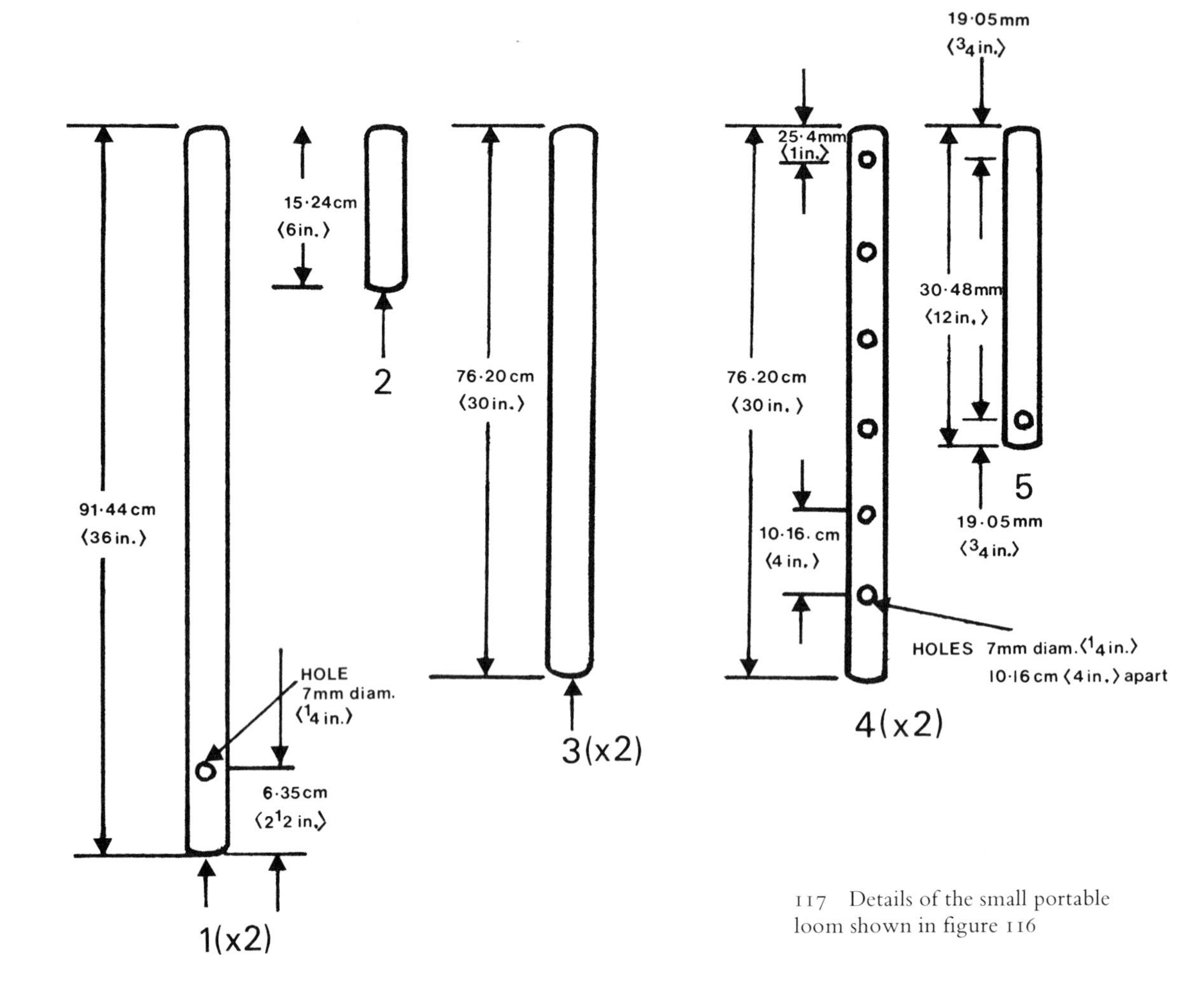

117 Details of the small portable loom shown in figure 116

MATERIAL LIST

QUANTITY	MATERIALS	DIMENSIONS (IMPERIAL)	DIMENSIONS (METRIC CONVERSIONS)	DETAILS
1	Elect conduit tube	12 ft × 1 in. diameter	365·76 cm × 25·4 mm diameter	1, 2, 3
1	Elect conduit tube	6 ft × $\frac{3}{4}$ in. diameter	182·88 cm × 19·05 mm diameter	4, 5
2	MS whit bolts	$\frac{7}{8}$ in. standard whit bolt × 6 in.	22·225 mm diameter standard whit thread × 15·24 cm	6
2	MS whit nuts	$\frac{7}{8}$ in. standard whit nuts	22·225 mm diameter × 22·225 mm thick	7
1	Wood dowel	6 ft × $\frac{5}{8}$ in. diameter	102·88 cm × 15·875 mm diameter	10, 11
1	MS square rod	2 ft × $\frac{1}{3}$ in. square	60·96 cm × 3·175 mm square	8
1	MS rod	3 ft × $\frac{27}{32}$ in. diameter	7·62 cm × 21·43 mm diameter	9
1	Plastic sleeving	6 in. × $\frac{1}{4}$ in. internal diameter	15·24 cm × 6·35 mm internal diameter	8
1	Strong cord	10 ft	3 metres	
1	Brass	6 in. × $\frac{1}{4}$ in. diameter	15·24 cm × 6·35 mm diameter	12
1	MS dowel	1 ft × $\frac{1}{8}$ in. diameter	30·48 cm × 3·175 mm diameter	
6	MS		2 BA csk. st. sc. × 12·7 mm	
4	MS		2 BA rd. hd. st. sc. × 12·7 mm	

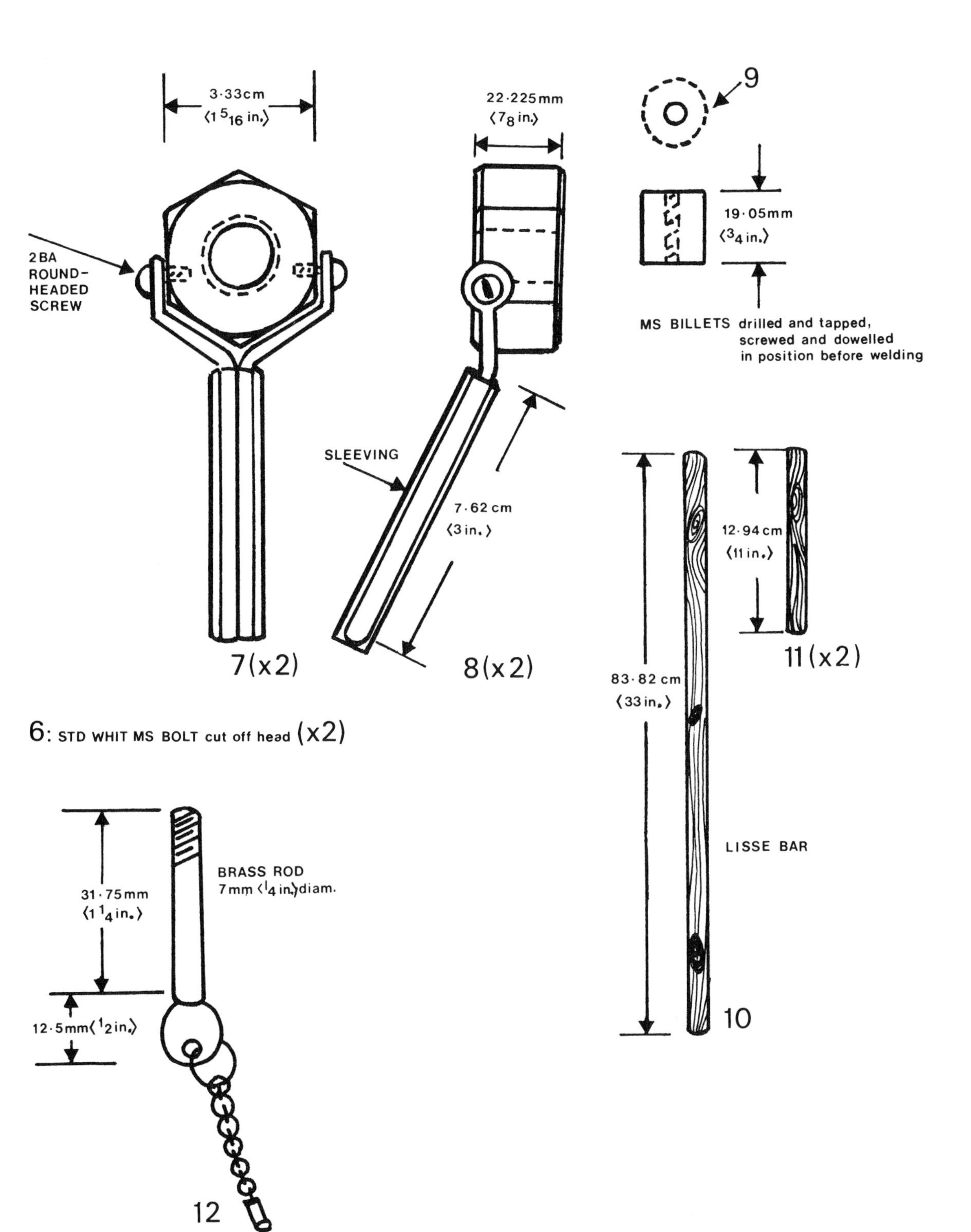
3·33cm
⟨1 5/16 in.⟩
2BA
ROUND-
HEADED
SCREW
7(x2)
22·225mm
⟨7/8 in.⟩
SLEEVING
7·62 cm
⟨3 in.⟩
8(x2)
9
19·05mm
⟨3/4 in.⟩
MS BILLETS drilled and tapped,
screwed and dowelled
in position before welding
12·94 cm
⟨11 in.⟩
11(x2)
83·82 cm
⟨33 in.⟩
LISSE BAR
10
6: STD WHIT MS BOLT cut off head (x2)
31·75mm
⟨1 1/4 in.⟩
BRASS ROD
7mm ⟨1/4 in.⟩diam.
12·5mm⟨1/2 in.⟩
12

Warping-up a simple frame

To fix the warp on a simple, small frame, it is first necessary to establish the length of the warp threads required by taking the length of the frame in the direction in which the warp is intended to run, doubling this length and adding an extra 50 cm to 76 cm (20 in. to 30 in.) for tying and possible wastage. This gives the length of a double warp thread, and the supply of warp material is then cut up into pieces of this length, as it is best to attach the warp threads to the frame double. They are attached by taking a double length of the warp material, folded into two, placing the looped end over and around one bar of the frame and pulling the ends of the thread through the loop to make a double-hitch knot. The loose ends of the warp thread are now taken over and around the bar at the opposite end of the frame, brought up one end on each side of the double warp threads and tied tightly in a reef knot over them. Make sure the knot is a reef knot and not a granny, or the warp threads will continually be coming loose (see figure 118). It is also necessary to see that the warp threads are evenly spaced and are at right-angles to the end bars of the frame. The tension of the warp threads must also be checked, not only before weaving begins, but also from time to time during weaving, as any unevenness of tension during weaving may cause an effect called rippling, where the more tightly stretched warp threads contract more than the others, after the finished piece of weaving is removed from the frame.

To calculate the number of warp threads to be attached to the frame, it is first necessary to discover how many threads of the chosen warp there are to every 25 mm (1 in.), when they are placed closely side by side. This number, if halved, will give the number of warp threads to every 25 mm (1 in.) that it is best to work with, when normal weft material is being used, as in these conditions the thickness of one thread should be left between all the warp threads on the frame. By measuring the particular design to be used, it is then possible to calculate how many warp threads altogether will need to be attached to the frame. If this number happens to be uneven, it is always possible to add one to it or subtract one from it, in order to warp up, as I have suggested, with double threads.

By adopting this method of using double warp threads for the initial warping-up, it is quite easy to achieve the correct spacing of the warp, if one makes sure that the loops, by which the double warps are attached to one end bar of the frame, are placed so that they just touch but do not overlap one another, nor leave spaces between one another along the bar. When the

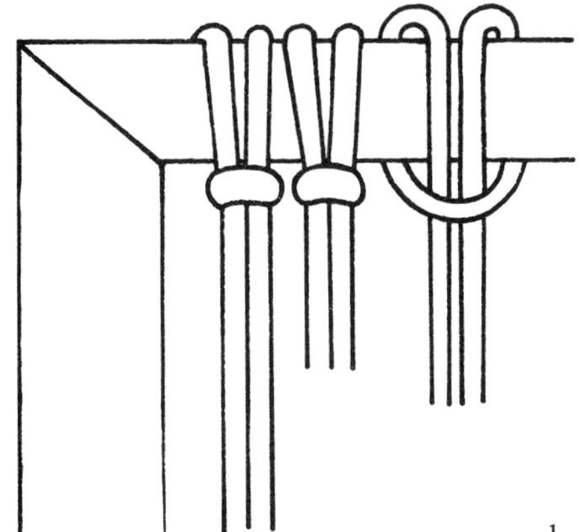

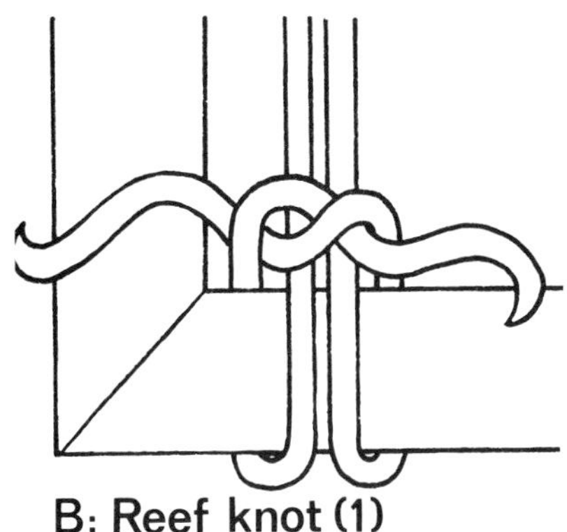

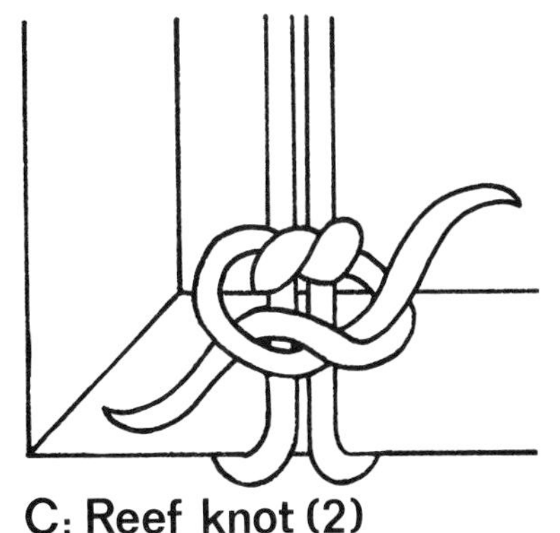

118 Warping-up a simple frame

double warps have been tied on and carefully spaced in this way, it is only necessary to weave about 12 mm ($\frac{1}{2}$ in.) of plain tapestry weave right across the full width of the warp and to press it down firmly, in order to separate the individual warp threads so that they are absolutely evenly spaced (see figure 86, page 76). This small piece of plain weaving can, if suitable, form part of the background of the finished piece, or it can be regarded as a selvedge, which can be turned under when the work is removed from the frame.

The warpstick should now be inserted through the warp threads by picking up all the uneven numbered threads and passing the stick under them until it stretches right across the whole width of the warp and rests upon the two side struts. Then, if the stick is placed upon its edge, it will form the shed through which the weft is passed one way. To form the reverse shed lisses (also called leashes or heddles) can be attached to the even numbered warp threads. These are pieces of thin twine about 152 mm (6 in.) long, which are used to encircle individual warp threads. The ends of the lisses are then knotted together and later they are joined together in pairs or, if the warp is a fine one, in threes or even in fours. The lisses enable the reverse shed to be formed by pulling them up with one hand whilst passing the weft through the warp shed with the other, but they are really only necessary if the design is fairly large, or if there are large areas of flat colour, such as plain background, to be worked. Otherwise, when working on small frames, it is generally easier just to pick up the warp threads with the needle or bobbin carrying the weft thread. Where lisses are used with a larger frame, such as the one shown in figure 116, where there is a rod to which they may be tied, then the length of twine needed for each lisse will have to be increased to about 50 cm (20 in.).

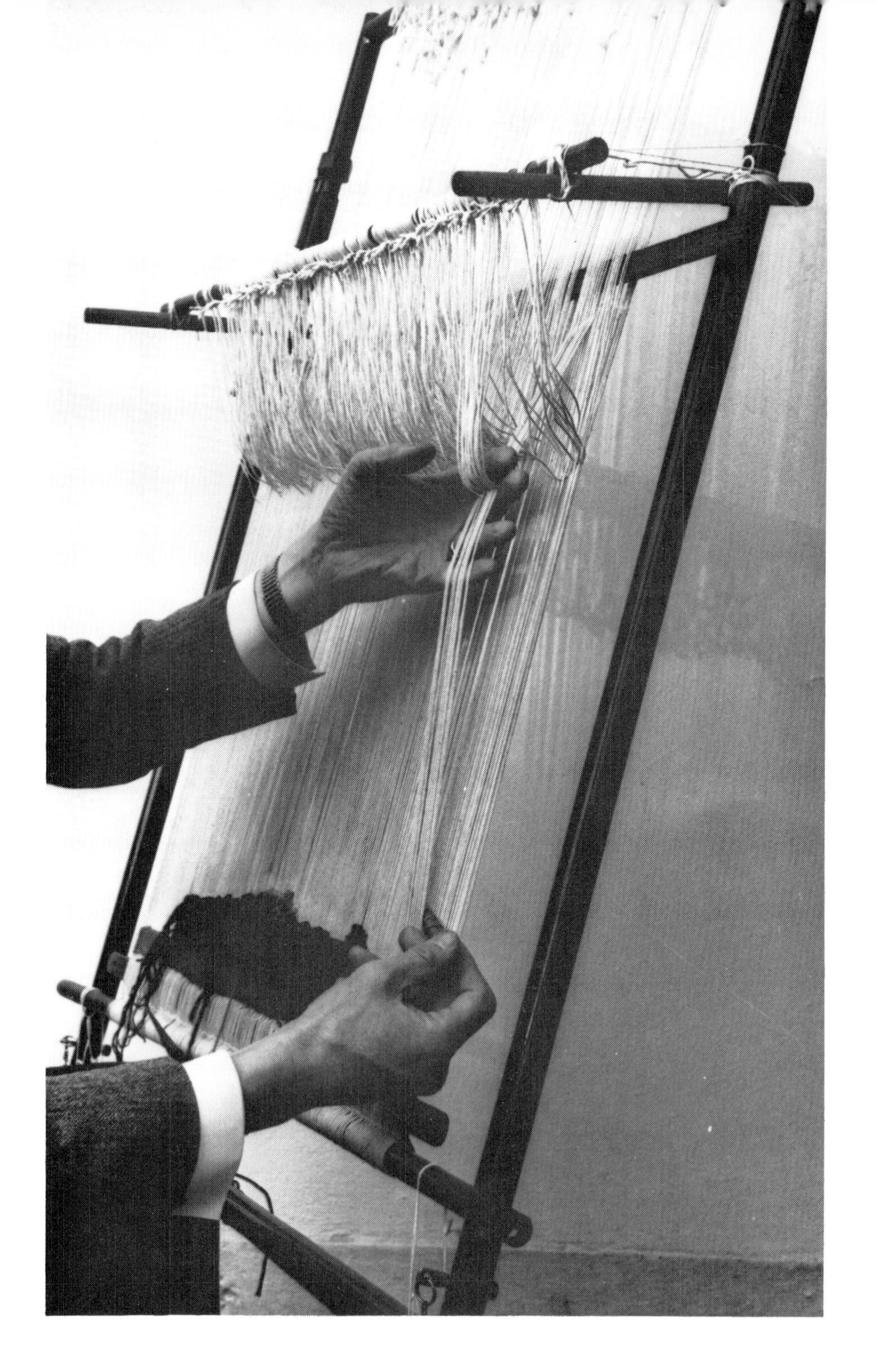

119 Lisses being used to form the reverse shed

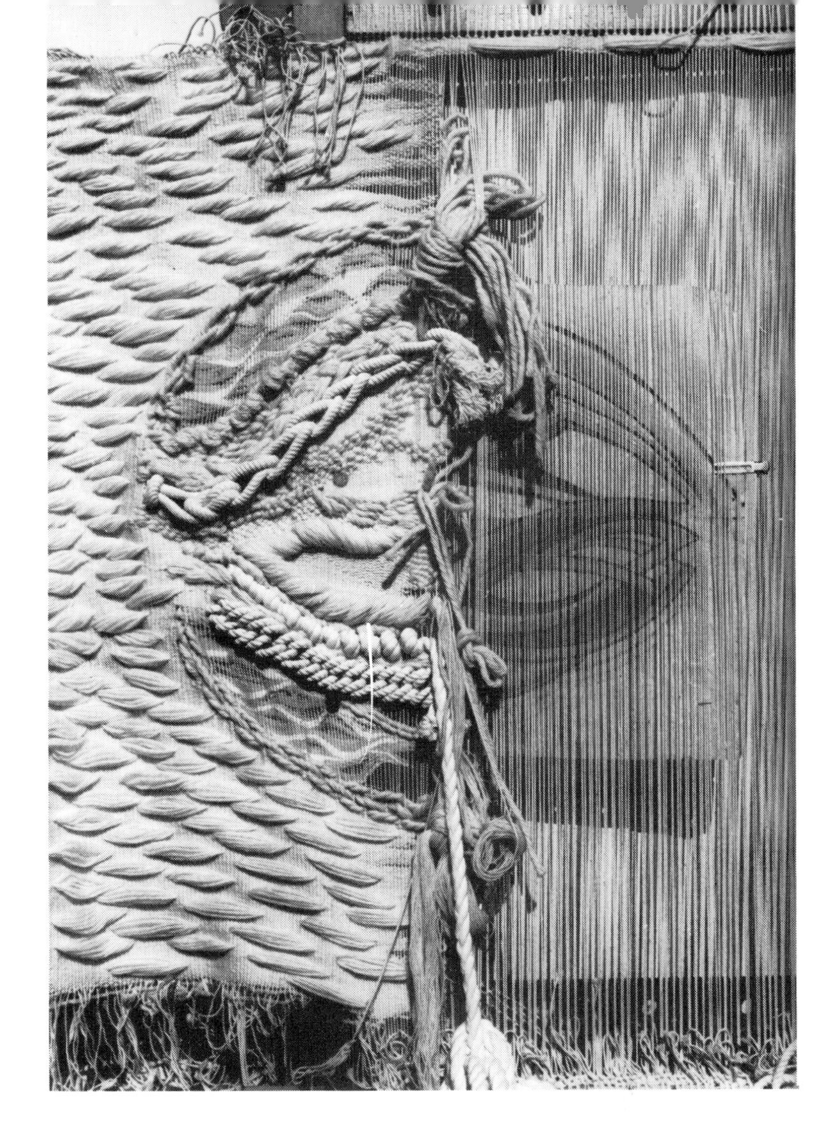

120 The second section of a larger tapestry panel is shown here about to be woven on a small frame. The completed first section has been moved to the side of the frame and new warp threads have been attached to the frame

Adding extra warp when weaving

When it is a question of weaving on a small frame a tapestry which needs a greater width of warp than the small frame can take, one section of the work can be completed first and then a further section of warp may be added. This is best done by removing the completed section of tapestry from the frame, re-attaching to the frame a few of the warp threads at the end of the completed piece, where the design is to be continued, and then adding some more warp to the frame. The new work should be keyed into the old section, and this is most easily done if some of the weft threads in the first section have not been taken right across to the final warp thread before the join (see figure 120).

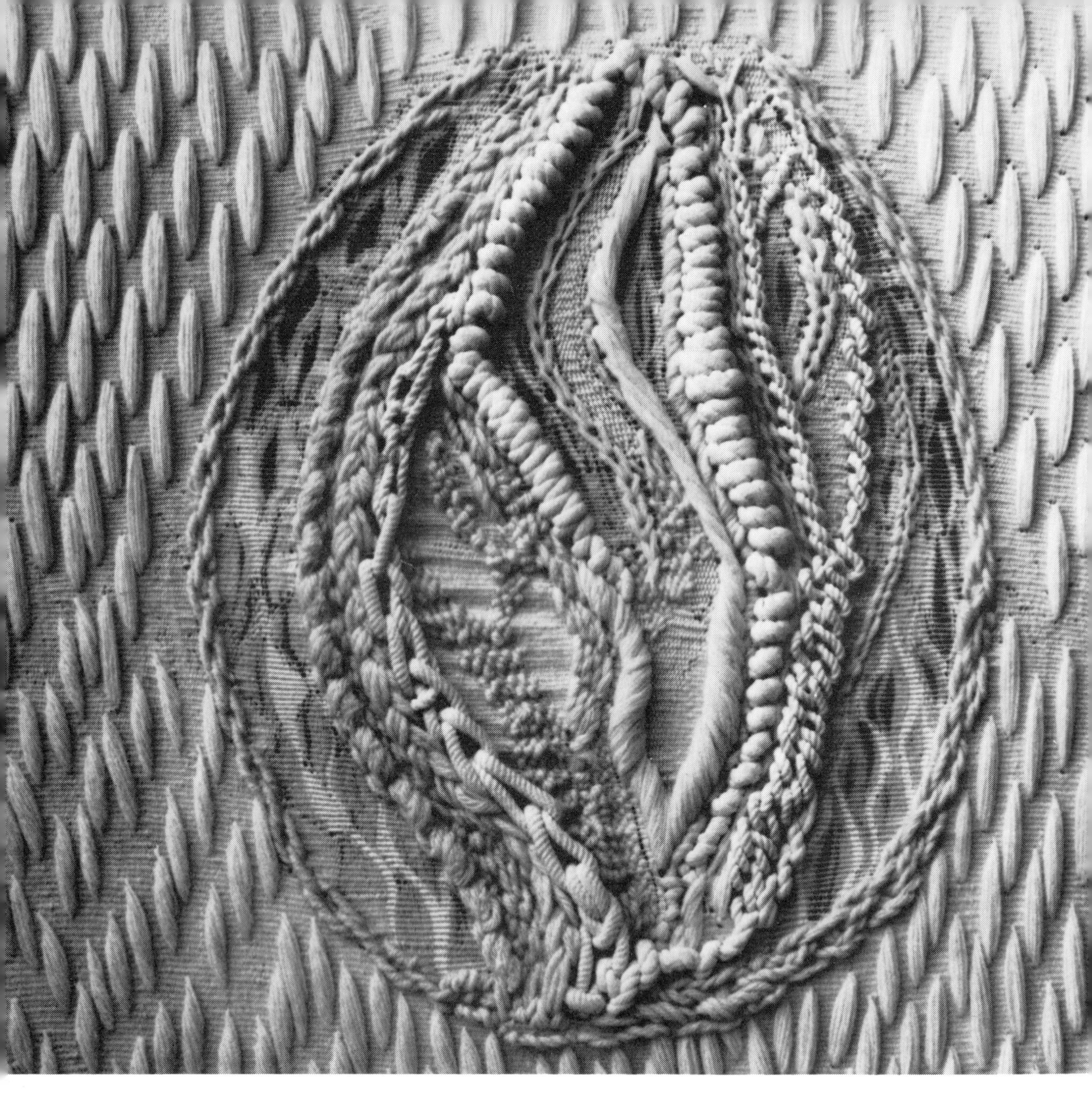

121 *Tropical Fruit* by *Mary Rhodes*. The completed panel previously shown in figure 120. It is woven in cream wool, with cream and white cords and some white cotton weft used to form the central motif. The background has a pattern of long weft threads left floating on the surface. It was found easier to work this panel from the front. The approximate dimensions are 84 cm × 76 cm (33 in. × 30 in.)

122 Detail of central motif of *Tropical Fruit*

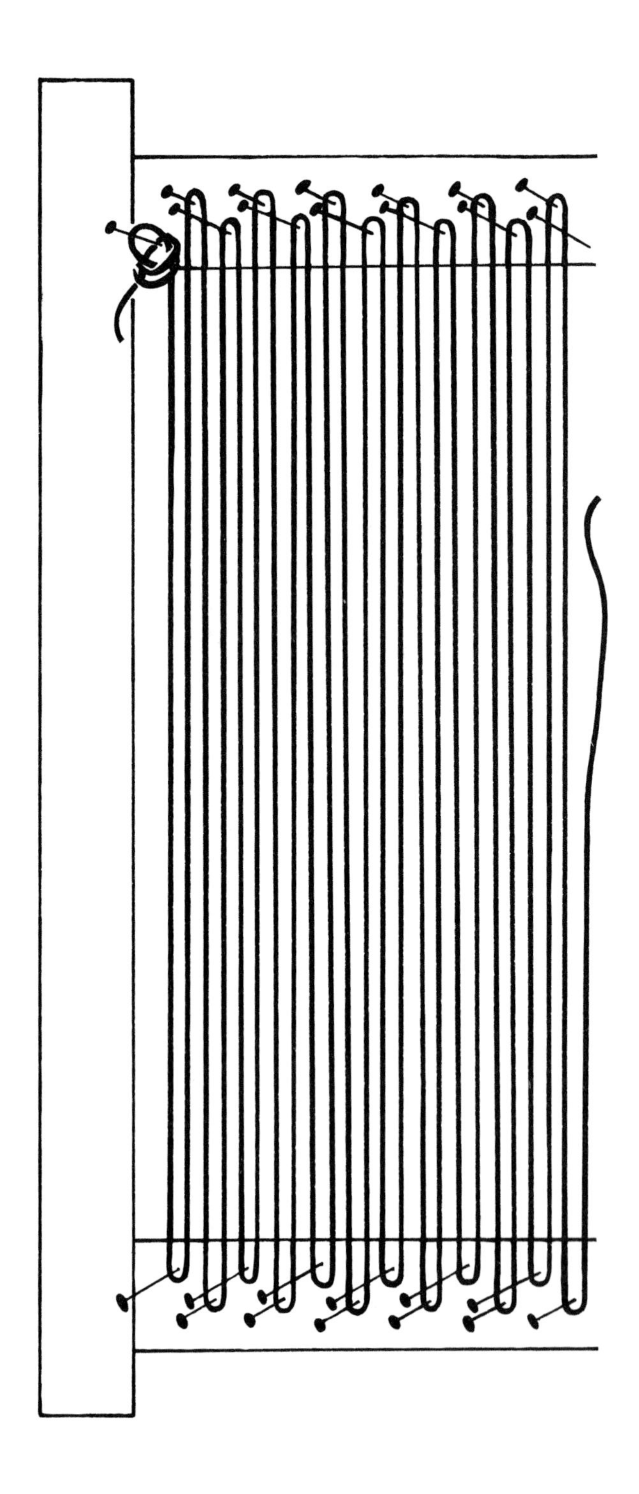

123 A nail frame, showing the method of tying on warp threads

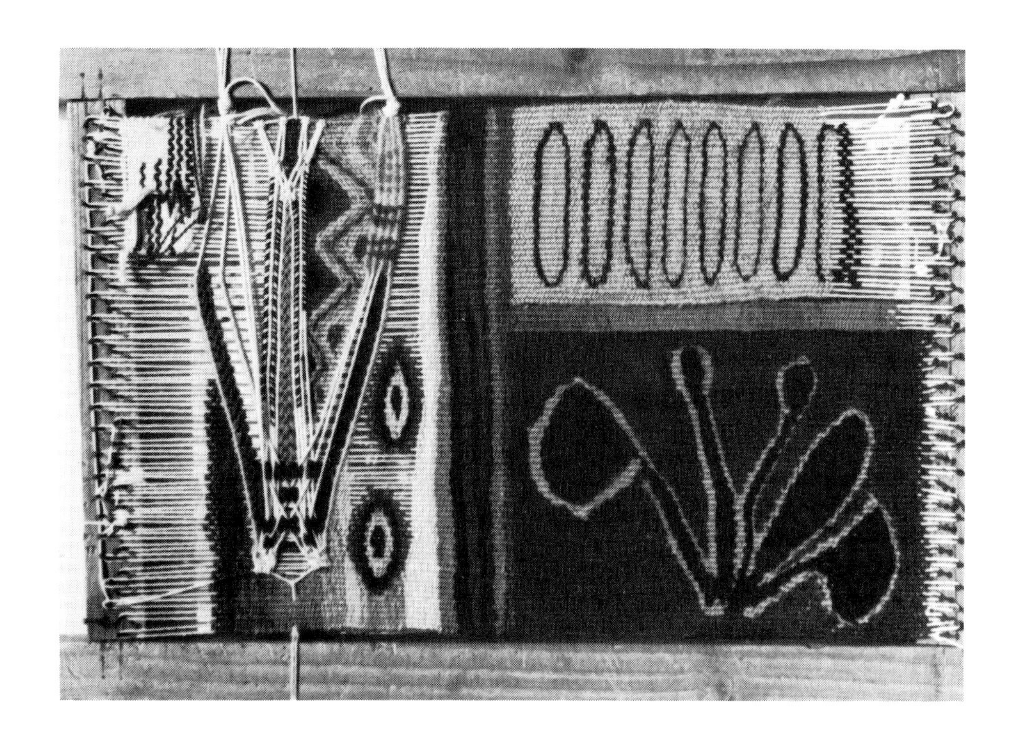

124 A nail frame being used for experimental weaving

The nail frame

This is a small, strong, rectangular wooden frame with two rows of small-headed nails inserted along each of two opposite sides, so that a sufficient length of each nail protrudes above the surface of the frame for the purpose of holding the warp thread in position. The nails are inserted at intervals of about 12 mm ($\frac{1}{2}$ in.) from one another, and the two rows on each side of the frame are staggered, as in figures 123 and 124.

One end of the warp is tied to the first nail and then the thread of the warp is taken backwards and forwards across the frame, first around the back nail, then around the front one on each side in succession. Finally the warp has to be tightened up to give a good, even tension in all the threads; then the end of the warp is tied firmly around the last nail.

When the tapestry has been completed, there should be enough elasticity in the warp to allow the loops around the nails to be pulled carefully over the heads of the nails without causing any damage to the work. If it is necessary to cut the loops in order to remove the work from the frame, the cut ends can either be simply knotted, or a neat finish can be given by turning back 6 mm ($\frac{1}{4}$ in.) of the work and stitching on a length of tape or webbing to cover the warp ends.

125 *Weed* by *Rennie Westmacott*. This piece of work measures approximately 40 cm × 61 cm ($15\frac{3}{4}$ in. × 24 in.). It was partly woven upon a rectangular frame, but the roundels, which were worked first, were woven on a circular loom, formed by the wooden end of a cheese carton. The roundels were then fixed to the background by being woven in as the work proceeded

A simple circular loom

Items such as embroidery rings, circular wooden ends of cheese cartons, strong circular pieces of card, notched around the edges, circles of perspex, a child's hoop or even a bicycle wheel rim can be used to make a simple loom on which to weave a circular panel of tapestry. The warp yarn is taken across the centre of the circular shape, the end having first been made fast to the edge somewhere, and it is either wrapped around the back of the shape before being brought across the centre in front again or, if the notched card or perspex disc is being used, the warp yarn is passed round behind one of the projections left between the notches on the edge and then brought back across the centre. Thus a basis of warp threads is formed, radiating out from the centre of the shape. There must be an uneven number of these warp threads so that when the weaving begins, as it does from the centre out towards the edge of the circle, as in a spider's web, the weft thread remains in the correct shed. If warp threads slip out of position during weaving, they can easily be adjusted and fixed back into place with a strip of *Sellotape,* which should be sufficient to hold them until the work is finished. Where the warp threads have been passed across the back of the circular shape as well as the front, two identical circular panels of tapestry can be woven if required.

126 Details of the roundels in figure 125, when first taken from the circular loom. The warp ends were wrapped in pairs after the roundels had been attached to the main panel

When the work is finished, it may be released from the circular loom, if the notched card or perspex has been used, by lifting the warp threads over the projections, but this does presuppose that the warp yarn is pliable enough. Where the warp has been carried across the back as well as the front of the loom, it can be freed by cutting the threads of warp around the edge of the shape.

127 A small circular panel of tapestry woven upon a wooden disc. The finished work has been retained upon the disc and embellished with feathers

The branch loom

A primitive type of small loom can be made from the branch of a tree. A small branch of pleasing shape should be chosen, which has a strong and firm main stem with side twigs which are pliant and capable of being bent into interesting shapes. When a satisfactory arrangement of the side twigs has been found, they should be tied into position, and threads of wool or cotton can then be tied across the spaces between them to form the warp. A design is hardly necessary for weaving on this loom, which offers a good opportunity for free experiment with a variety of warp and weft yarns of different thicknesses and many colours. The use of coloured warp makes it possible to leave certain sections of the warp uncovered and, as the finished work will, of course, remain permanently upon the loom, an attractive appearance can also be given to it by wrapping the branch and its twigs with yarns of various colours.

In choosing suitable branches for this purpose, it is desirable to find wood which is strong and in good condition, so that it does not become excessively brittle later. If, however, a chosen branch does break during weaving, extra twigs can be added by the process of wiring them on to the existing twigs with very thin wire. This wire will be covered, if the twigs are then wrapped with an attractive weft yarn.

Such a simple loom can prove quite exciting to experiment with and it can yield highly unusual effects. It is also particularly useful for children to learn on, when they become interested in weaving, for it is not an expensive piece of apparatus, but one which can be easily acquired by looking around the garden or keeping one's eyes open on a country walk.

Working on a continuous warp

A cardboard or plastic tube can become a loom with a continuous warp. A length of warp yarn has one end attached to the top edge of the tube and is then wound around the tube so that an evenly-spaced series of warp threads is formed along the whole length of the tube. The other end of the warp thread is then attached to the bottom end of the tube, and a piece of *Sellotape* is stuck over the warp threads from the top to the bottom of the tube in a straight line to hold the warp in position, and also to act as a base upon which to knock down the weft. Weft threads are inserted through the warp and woven from top to bottom of the tube as shown in figure 129. A design is not really needed for a piece of work of this kind, but one could be drawn on the tube before warping-up and would be clearly

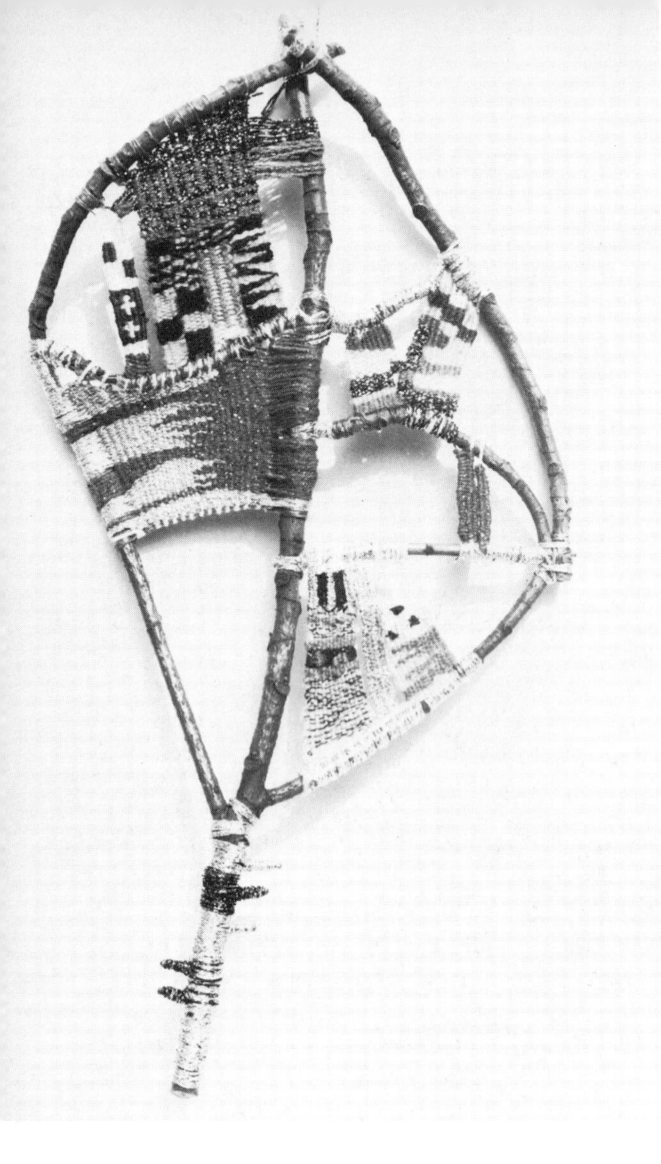

128 (LEFT) Branch loom. A small branch has been bent and tied into an attractive shape. It has then been warped and woven on in places

129 (RIGHT) Working on a continuous warp. A single thread of warp has been wrapped around a cardboard tube until it covers the entire exterior with the warp evenly spaced. The ends of the thread are fixed down and weaving has been commenced with woollen weft. When finished, this could form an attractive and unusual base for a table lamp

visible through the warp threads. When completed, the piece of tapestry can easily be removed from the tube, and it could be used as part of a free-standing woven construction. Its most obvious use, however, if the work is retained on the tube, is as a table lamp-base.

6 *Finishing and mounting woven tapestry*

When the weaving of a rectangular panel of tapestry has been completed, the edges of the work, where the weft begins and ends, should be oversewn with a suitable weft material to hold the first and last threads of the weft firmly in position, and prevent any unravelling. This oversewing should be done to a depth of two weft threads and should pass through alternate spaces between the warp threads (see figure 140). The tapestry can then be removed from the frame by first untying the reef knots holding the warp in position at one end and then cutting the double-hitch knots at the other end of the frame.

Such small rectangular tapestries, whether woven with the warp running horizontally or vertically across the finished surface, are often mounted on a wooden frame or stretcher, which needs to be slightly larger than the woven panel. The warp ends are used for tying two sides of the tapestry to the stretcher, whilst the other two sides are laced on to it with suitable strong twine, and by this means the work can be stretched and given a smooth surface. Then, if desired, the whole thing can be framed: a wooden frame which is deep enough to cover the stretcher and the knotted warp ends can be used or, as we have found among my group of students, pieces of strip-aluminium can easily be cut and fitted to cover the stretcher frame and will give the work a neat and pleasing finish. Tapestries should, however, not be glazed.

Another very suitable way of finishing and mounting a tapestry panel after the oversewing has been completed is to cut back the ends of the warp threads to about 50 mm (2 in.) in length and to turn them under to the back of the work, sewing a length of tape or webbing over them for neatness. If the tape or webbing is sewn along all four edges at the back of the tapestry, rings can be stitched on to the tape or webbing along the top edge and these can be used for hanging the work. The webbing itself can also be used to make loops through which a rod or length of flat wood or metal can be put for hanging purposes.

Small tapestries are often woven today which are not rect-

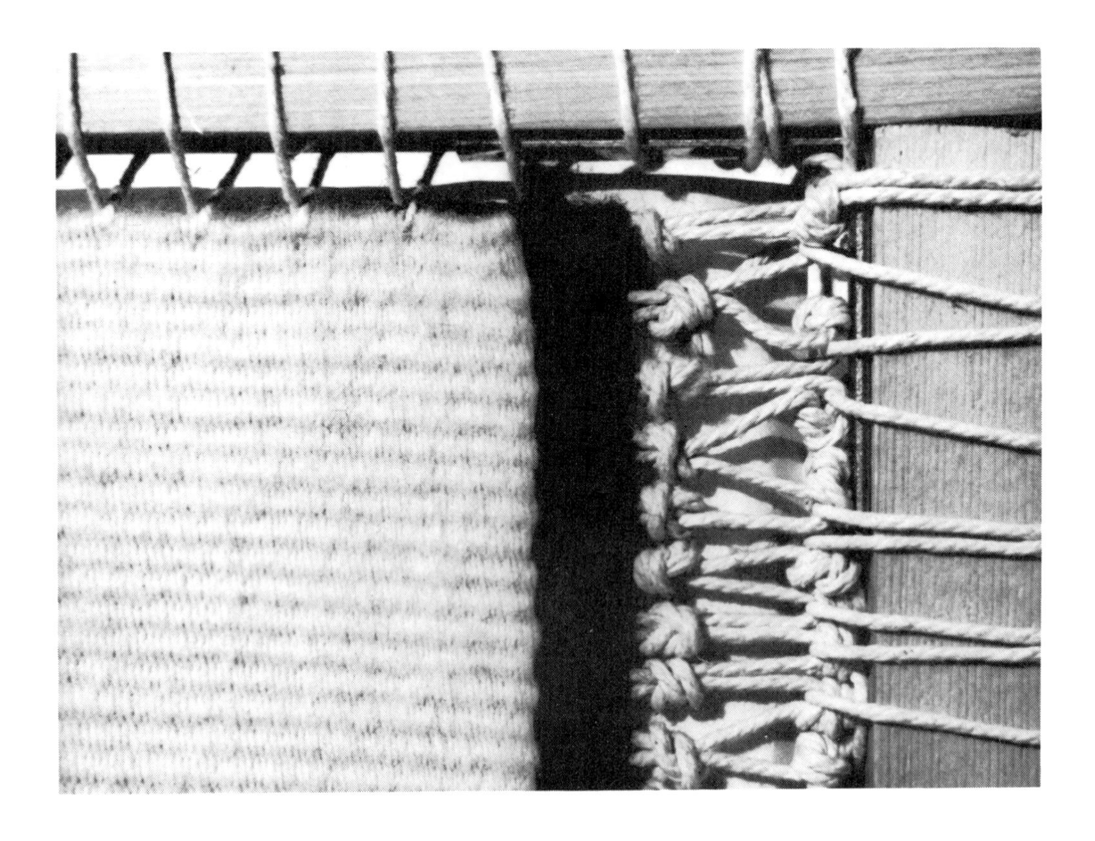

angular in shape and are unsuitable for framing in the way just mentioned. They are often pieces in which the warp runs vertically across the finished surface and may not be fully covered by the weft. These pieces can present quite a problem, and we have to look for the best method of finishing them off which will make it easy to hang them and at the same time enhance the appearance of the work. Happily, there are many attractive ways of dealing with the matter. A tapestry with vertical warp, especially where the lower edge of the weaving does not form a straight line at right-angles to the sides of the work, but is irregular or undulating, can have the lower ends of the warp threads knotted in various decorative ways. In this connection a knowledge of macramé knotting can prove very useful, and may provide some exciting ways of finishing off a tapestry wall-hanging. Bobbles of unspun wool can also be tied on to a group of warp ends, as is done by the Tunisians when finishing-off their woven blankets, or the ends can be wrapped

130 This shows the knotting of warp ends together in pairs and the lacing of a rectangular panel to a wooden stretcher

131 Hand-made bobbles, fixed to a panel with continuous warp

with a variety of gaily-coloured weft materials. Sometimes the wrapped warp ends can be plaited quite effectively, or simply left looped together, but more exciting results may be achieved by attaching to them such things as feathers, seed-heads, shells, pieces of fur, large beads, curtain rings, small metal discs or washers and things like peach stones or small pebbles enclosed in a sling. It is often a good idea to wrap groups of warp ends together before embellishing them in this way (see figures 131–43).

At the top of such an irregularly shaped tapestry the warp ends probably do not need to be so decoratively treated, as the main object here is to find a suitable means by which the work can be hung. If it is not possible to turn the warp ends to the back of the work, then the best suggestion will probably be to wrap them and form them either into a number of loops through which a rod may be passed for hanging, or into one large loop which can be used for the same purpose.

132 (OPPOSITE ABOVE) Tassels made from various threads, attached by means of a finger-made chain to a tapestry with a continuous warp

133 (OPPOSITE BELOW) Hand-made tassels of cotton perlé

134 Detail of *Merlin,* showing wrapped warp ends, finished off with seed-heads of the magnolia *grandiflora*

135 Decorative, wrapped warp ends beside warp ends embellished with small bundles of wool. The latter were wrapped with brightly coloured silk and cotton

136 Knotted warp ends

137 (LEFT) Metal washers, fastened to the ends of the warp and left uncovered, can look most attractive and unusual

138 (RIGHT) A method of finishing off warp ends by attaching them to covered curtain rings

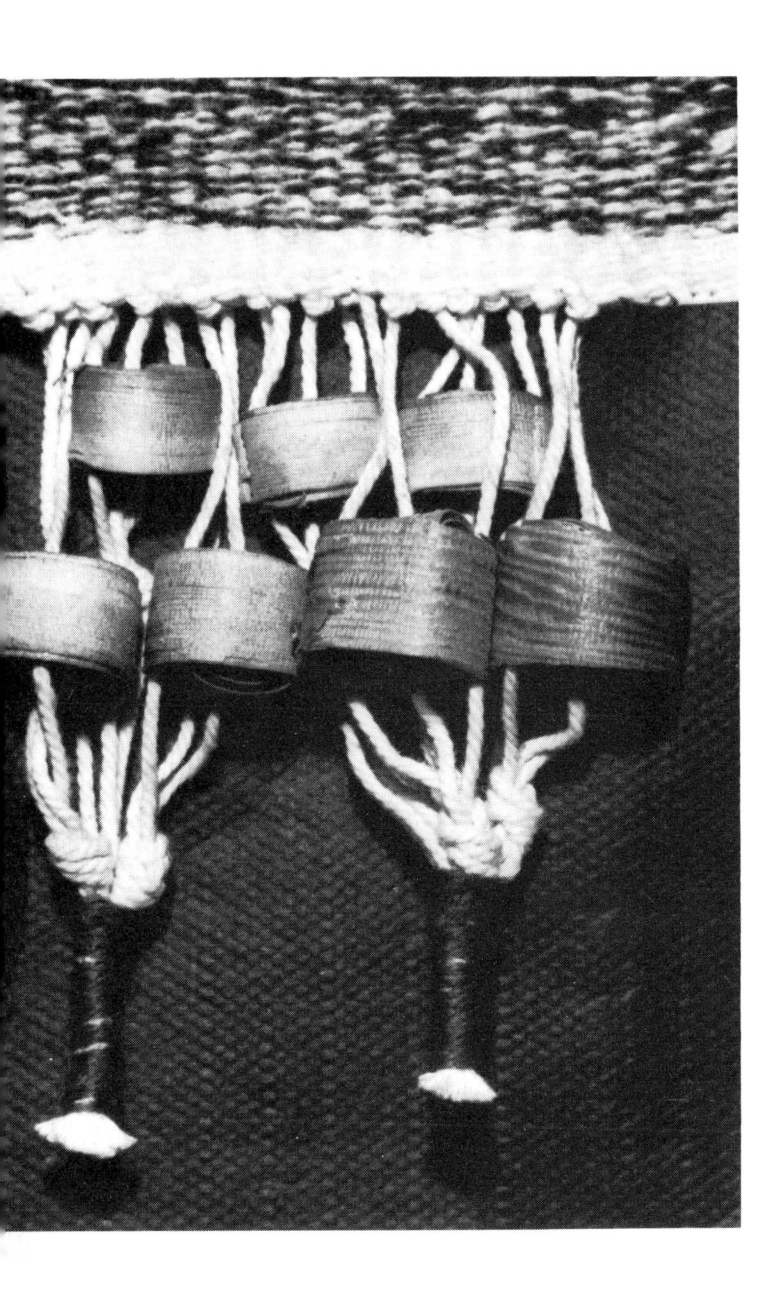

139 Curled wood shavings fixed on to warp ends, which have then been knotted and finally wrapped

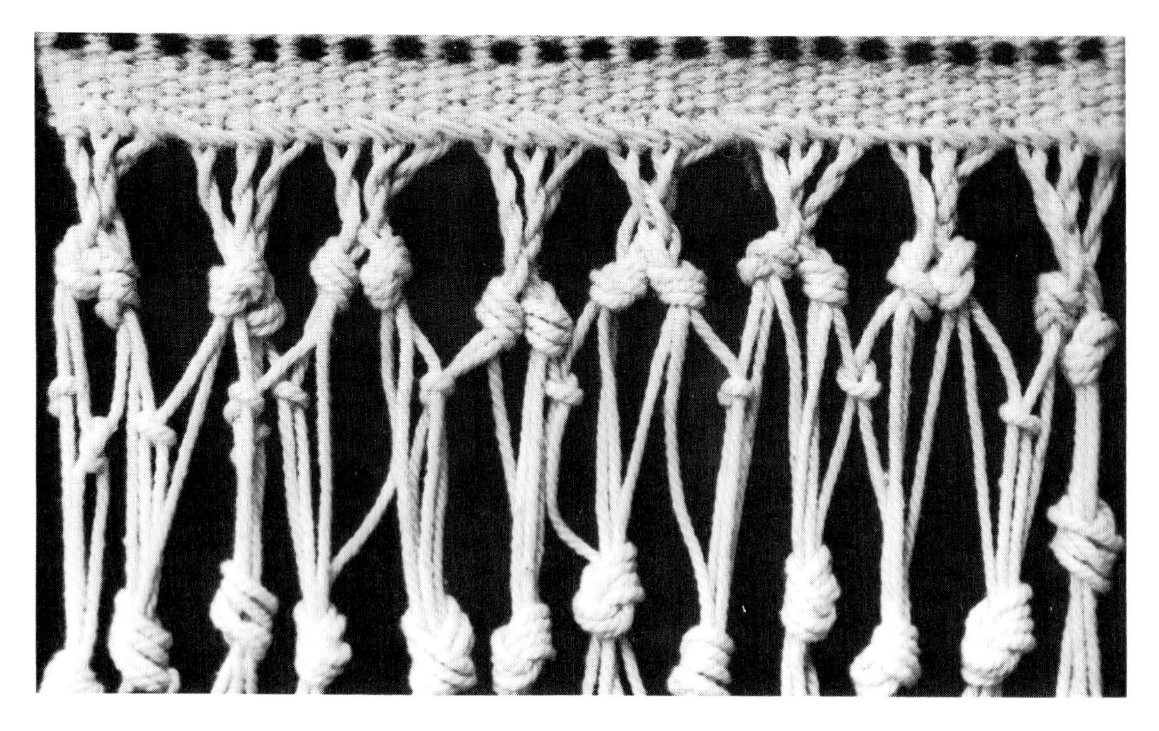

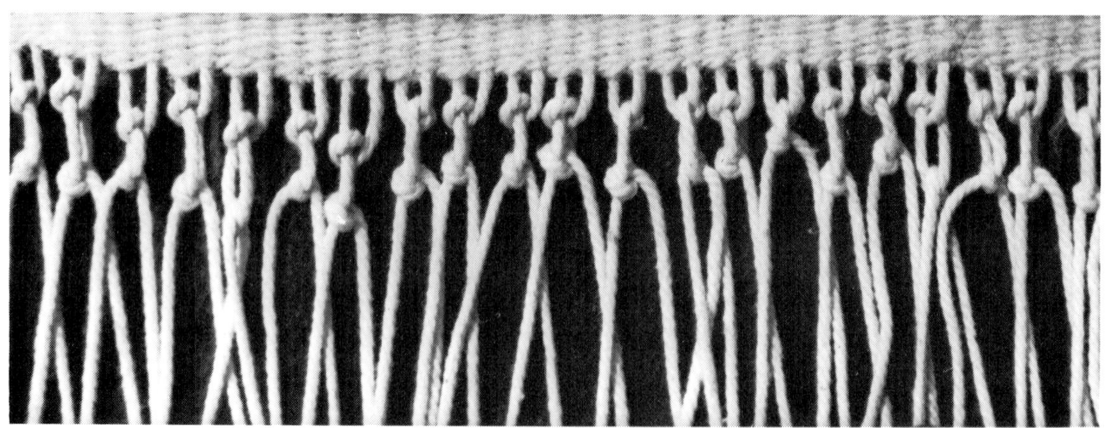

140 (ABOVE) Oversewing the selvedge and a way of knotting the warp ends

141 (BELOW) A simple way of knotting warp ends

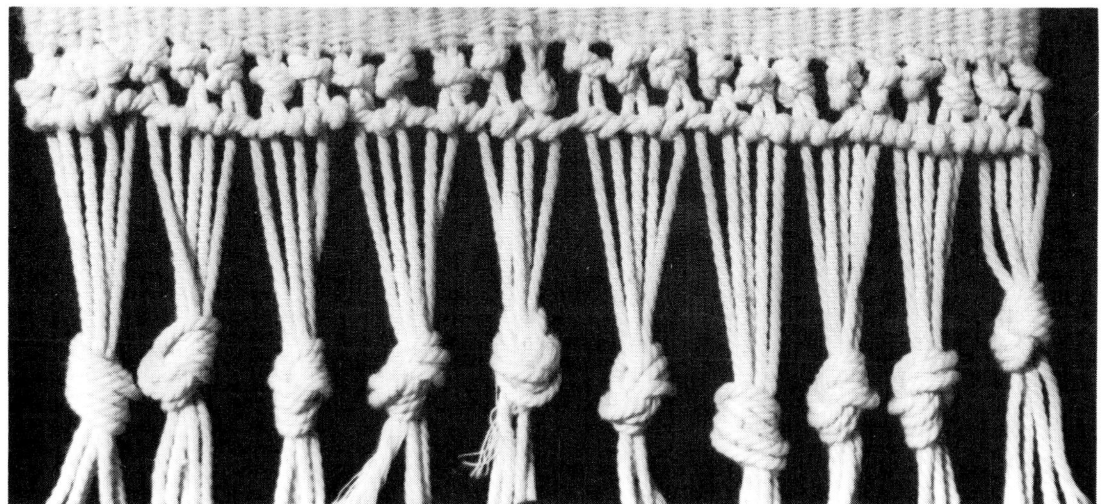

142 (ABOVE) Warp ends plaited and then knotted

143 (BELOW) Another way of knotting warp ends

144 *City in the Sun* by *Val Rhodes*. A small tapestry, 47 cm ($18\frac{1}{2}$ in.) square, worked in wool and silk. Vertical lines in blue, black, white and green suggest shapes of buildings against a large orange sun. The effect of reflections in water is given by areas of blue, hatched into the white background, at either side of the panel

145 *Trees* by *Nellie Old.* A small well-woven piece, which exploits very skilfully the special characteristics of tapestry technique

146 *Flower Child* by *Jacqueline Fern*. A long panel woven on coarse string warp with wool and cotton, in a rich colouring of yellow, rust, magenta, green and blue

147 *Frogs* by *May Hards*

Conclusion

Having had for many years a deep interest in the fascinating art-form of woven tapestry, and having also been practically concerned in its production, I have endeavoured to bring together in this book some ideas gained from my experience which I hope will encourage ordinary people—and especially young people—who are as yet unacquainted with the craft, to start weaving pictorial tapestries. I should also like to hope that those who are already highly skilled in hand weaving, but who have not yet experienced the freedom and the pleasure to be found in tapestry weaving, might be inspired by this book to experiment in the same direction.

148 *Deer* by *Miriam Bawden*. A beautifully woven panel with lines of weft running diagonally to the warp direction, in an endeavour to depict shafts of sunlight

149 *Abstract Panel* by *Doris Warans*. ▶ An abstract design woven in black, red and orange wool on coarse cotton warp

150 A partly woven panel in silk and wool, the design of which shows the influence of tapestries by modern French designers, such as Jean Lurçat.

Bibliography

A Short History of Tapestry
Eugène Müntz, Cassell London, 1885

The Practical Book of Tapestries
George Leland Hunter, J. B. Lippincott Philadelphia & London, 1925

The Art of Tapestry
Edited by Joseph Jobé, Thames & Hudson London, 1965

Tapisseries de Jean Lurçat 1939–1957
Pierre Vorms, Éditeur d'Art a Belvès Dordogne, 1957

French Tapestry
Edited by André Lejard, Paul Elek London, 1946

Textiles of Ancient Peru and their Techniques
Raoul d'Harcourt, University of Washington Press, 1962

The Technique of Woven Tapestry
Tadek Beutlich, Batsford London; Watson-Guptill New York, 1967

Designing Tapestry
Jean Lurçat, Rockliff London

A History of Tapestry
W. G. Thomson, Hodder and Stoughton London, 1906

Contemporary Tapestry
Harriet Tidball, Shuttle Craft Monograph Twelve, 1964
Distributed by Craft and Hobby Service, Big Sur, California

Creative Design in Wall Hangings
Lili Blumenau, George Allen and Unwin London, 1967

Swedish Weaving
Edited by Thelma M. Nye, Batsford London; Van Nostrand Reinhold New York, 1972

Creative Textile Craft—Thread and Fabric
Rolf Hartung, Batsford London; Van Nostrand Reinhold New York, 1964

Flemish Weaving
Gertrud Ingers, Van Nostrand Reinhold New York, 1971

Index

Figures in *italics* refer to illustrations